Chincoteague – Assateague Seaside Adventure

*Live in the sunshine,
swim the sea,
drink the wild air.*

Ralph Waldo Emerson

This book, Chincoteague-Assateague Seaside Adventure, is a unique memory book that captures the highlights of an Island vacation. Through pictures and short prose, readers can experience a visit to Chincoteague and Assateague Islands, showcasing the beauty and nature available in every season.

Jonathan & Jane Richstein
Sundial Books
4065 Main Street
Chincoteague, VA 23336
757-336-5825

Chincoteague – Assateague Seaside Adventure

A Photo-Journey Guide

Yaakov Gridley

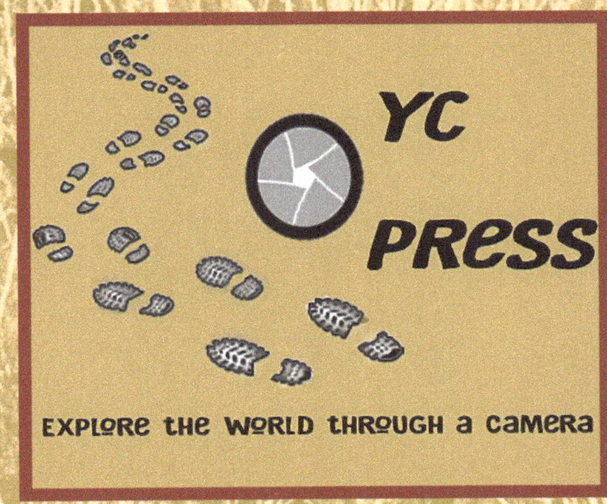

Copyright

YC Press

6019 Neilwood Drive, Suite 100, Rockville, MD 20852

Library of Congress Control Number: 2020911358

ISBN 978-1-7341774-3-5

Dedication

To my wife and best friend, Glo, whose love and support made this project possible—I am ever indebted. And to my parents, the well-spring of all my creativity.

— Yaakov Gridley

Acknowledgment

To Marcia Lewis, for editing this book, and to Rob Young, ornithologic specialist, for identifying the birds.

About Yaakov

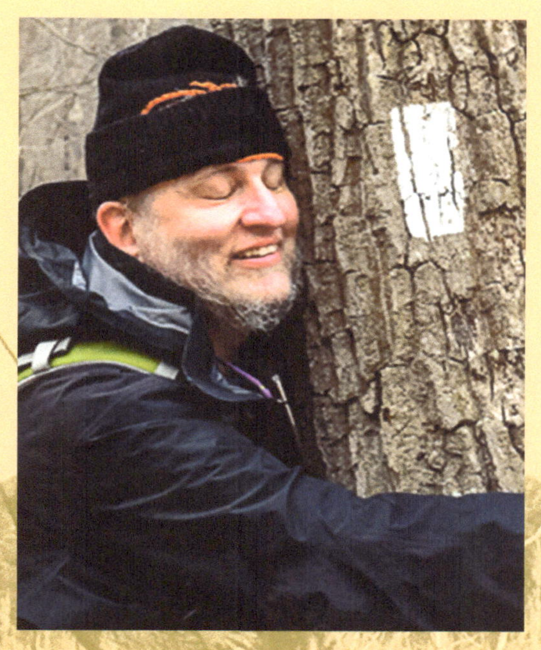

You might not be surprised to learn that I'm a tree-hugger from way back, but I appreciate beauty both in nature and in art. I have had a life-long love of both photography and adventure, and I bring these two together to explore a world that is both insulated and accessible to any who want to get away from the hubbub of city life.

To appreciate the wide range of my adventures, you may wish to enjoy exploring my website at www.photojourneys.org. This book is the first in my *Photo-Journey Guide* series, in which I walk you through my adventures that are not only wondrous but also close at hand. I've also created unpublished travel books on subjects such as cruising the Caribbean islands, and I'm planning more *Photo-Journey Guide* series books in the future. Soon to be published: *Sugarloaf Mountain Near Washington, DC.*

Contents

Prologue

My wife and I have visited the Chincoteague and Assateague islands for many years. Most years we visited in the summer, and later also at Thanksgiving. This book covers such a week-long visit. The sights, of course, are the same for any season.

I enjoy both the summer and the autumn, and you can make up your own mind which is best. In the autumn, the kids, the crowds, and the bugs are gone. The fast-foods and putt-putt are closed. And Chincoteague is a quiet little rural town again.

In every season, however, nature is in full gear here. We love the shore birds and the migratory birds. We share the beach and ponds with photographers and birders. And of course we enjoy the wild ponies.

There is now an additional attraction: the lighthouse. Previously it was closed to the public, but it is now available for tourists to climb its steps and to enjoy the exceptional view from the top.

Finding Your Way: Chincoteague Island and Assateague Island

Chincoteague Island is the residential area (opposite page, left side), while Assateague Island (opposite page, right side) is not inhabited, but is the location of the Chincoteague National Wildlife Refuge. There are sandy beaches on Assateague Island and wild and lush marshes on both islands. Visiting Chincoteague Island is free, but access to Assateague Island is not, because it's a national park. There's a toll plaza just after the bridge.

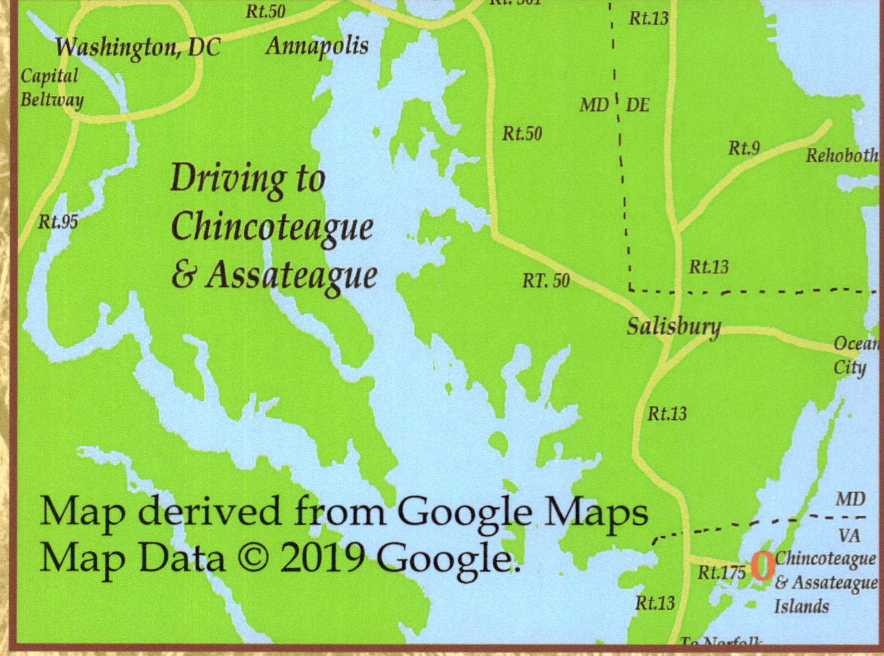

Map derived from Google Maps Map Data © 2019 Google.

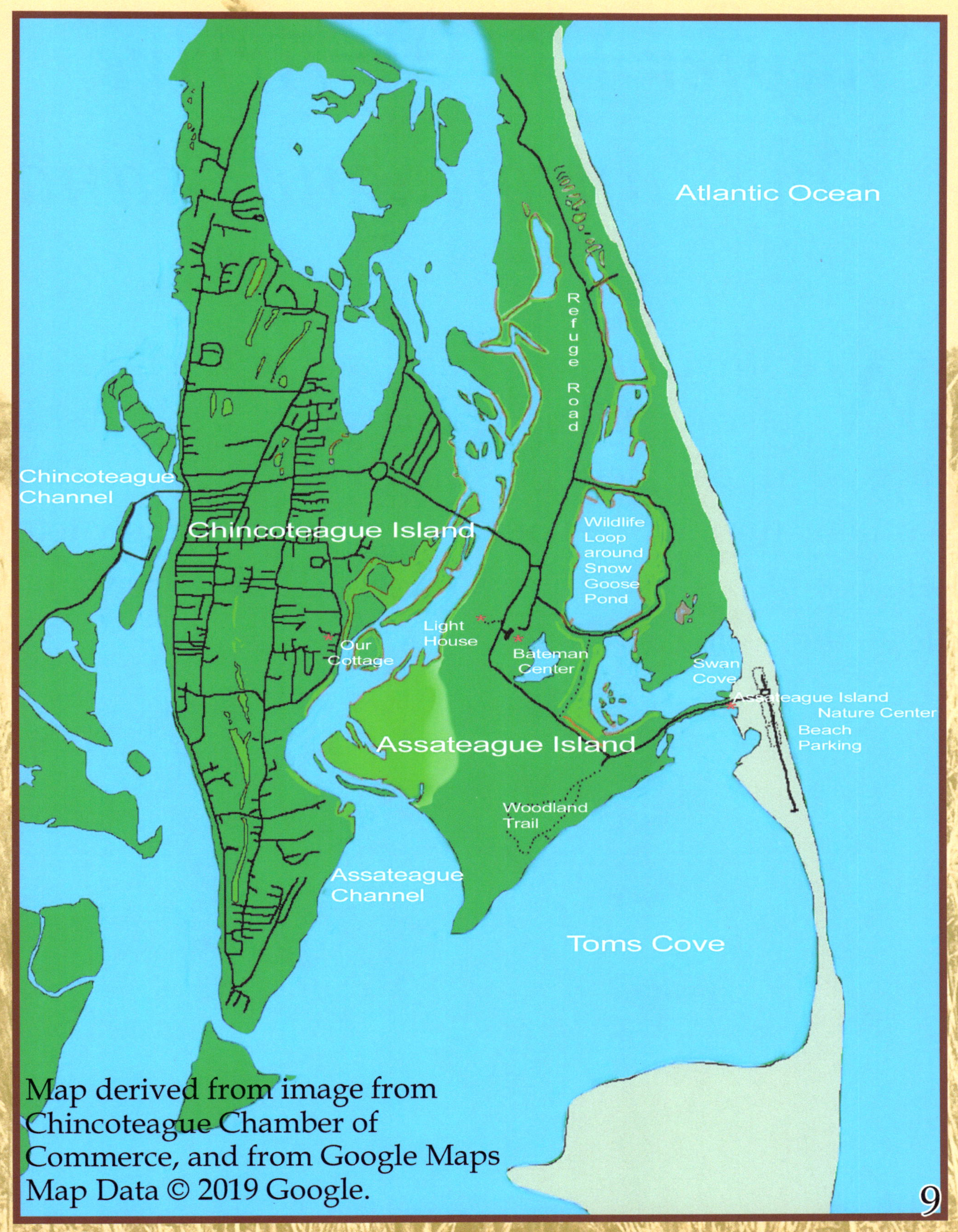

Map derived from image from Chincoteague Chamber of Commerce, and from Google Maps Map Data © 2019 Google.

9

Chapter 1 -- We Arrive On Chincoteague Island

We arrive late in the day, and by the time we get to our Chincoteague cottage (really a sort of garden apartment), it is dark, including inside the cottage, until we feel our way to some light switches. It's also a little musty; nostalgic to those who love the shore.

We walk around to the east side of the building, farthest from the road. Assateague Channel is lapping at the shore, and we hear ducks quacking in the dark. A light blinks "welcome" in the distance across the channel, but discovering the identity of this light will need to wait till morning.

Chapter 2 -- Discovering Chincoteague Island

We wake early and see this view when looking out the door that faces Assateague Channel.

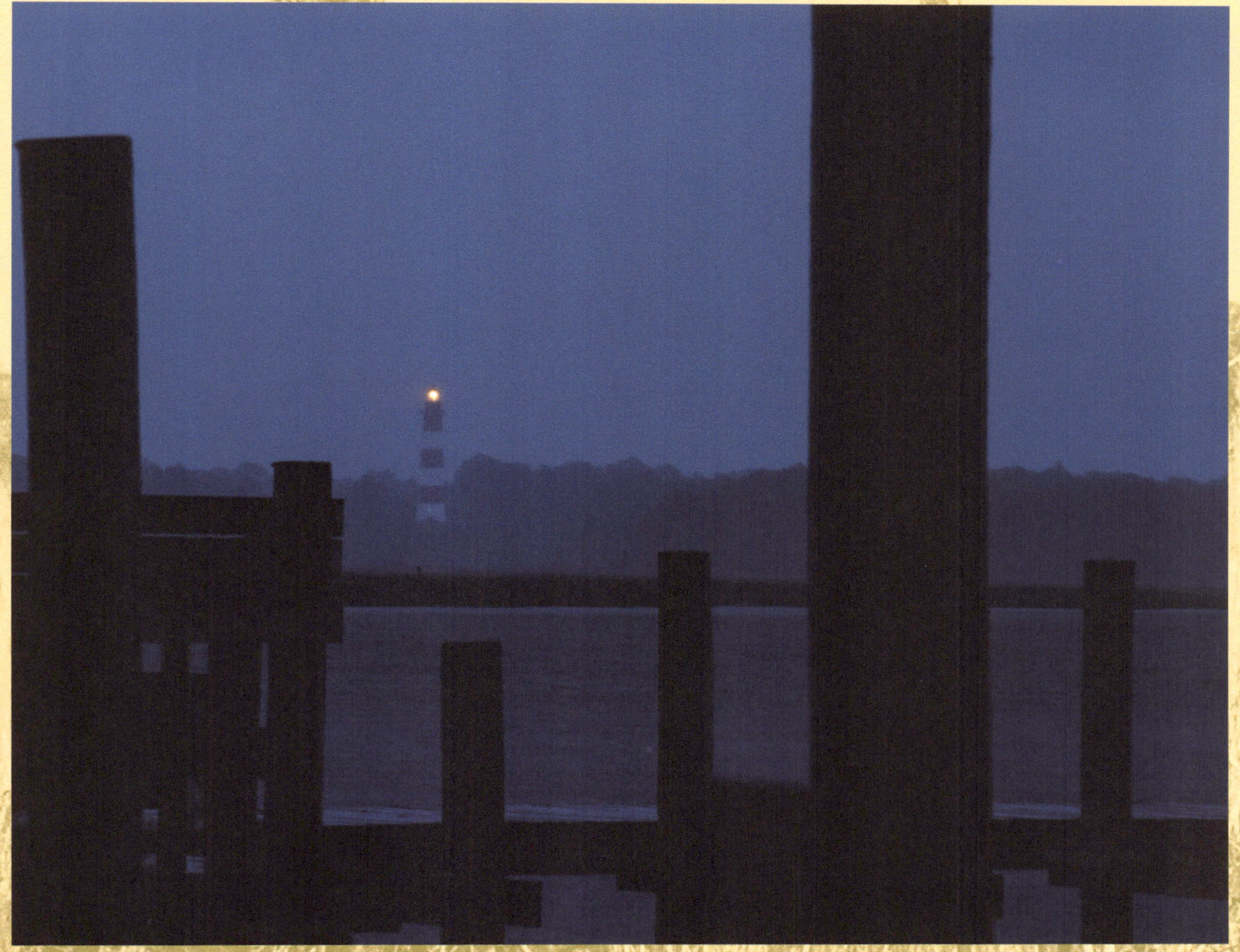

And from the porch at this door, we see the blinking light — it's the Assateague Lighthouse, bravely warning mariners of the dangerous shoals. We also discover something else — the sky is heavily overcast. Is it always like this?

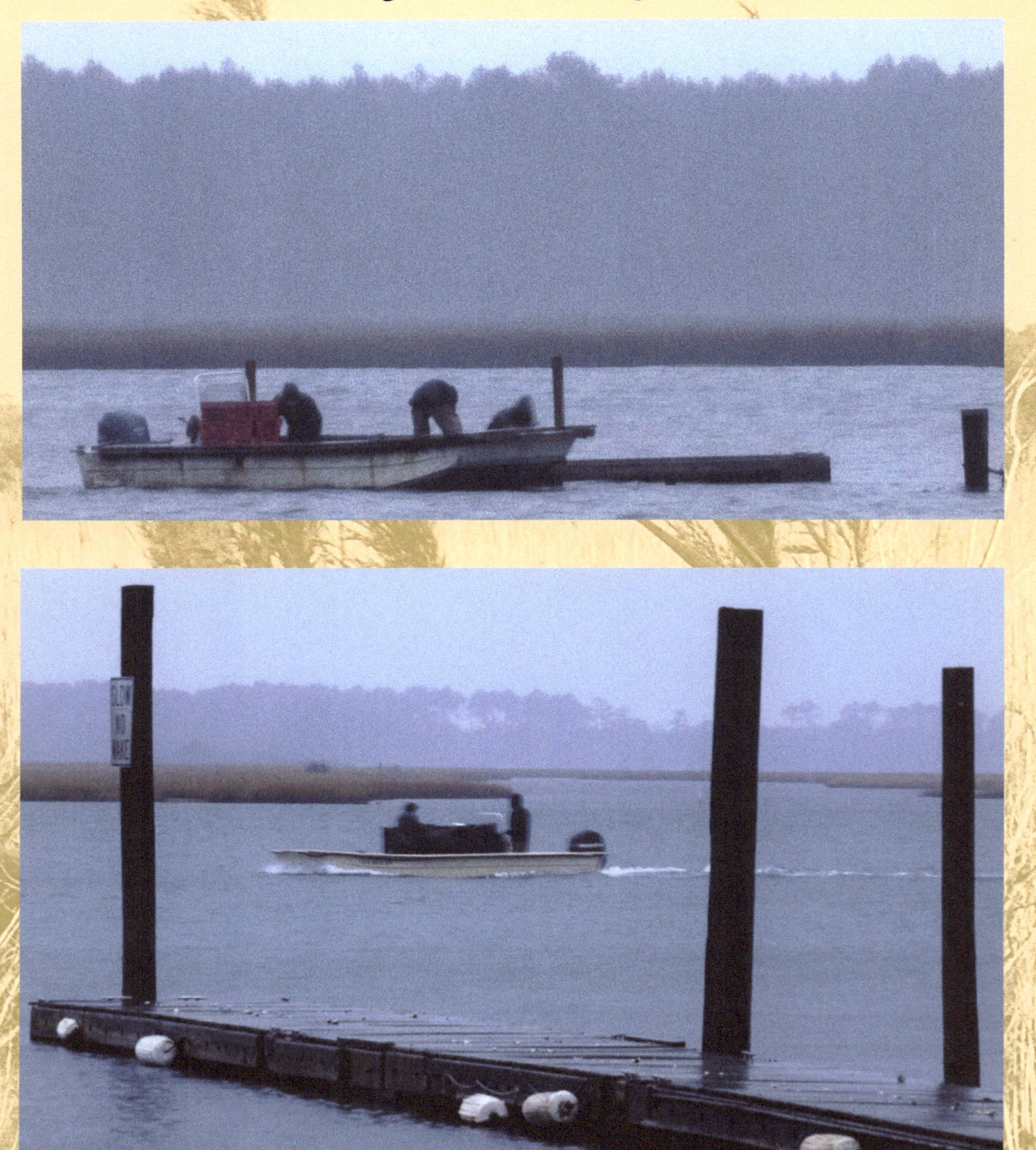

Fishermen show up early in the morning, do their work, and then depart.

Chincoteague & Assateague

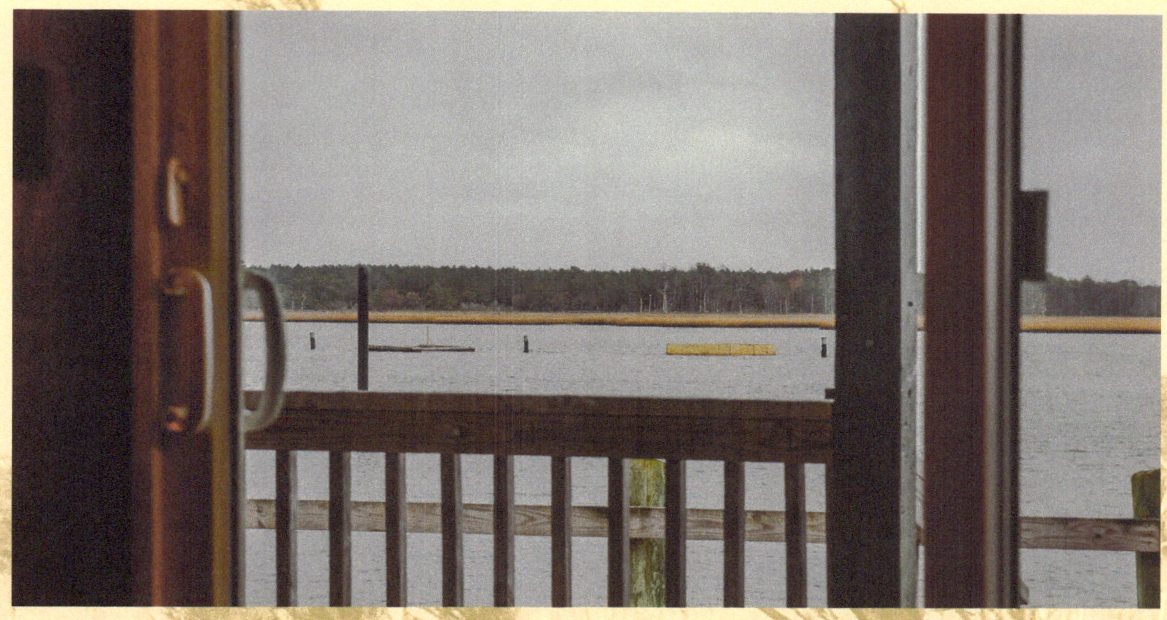

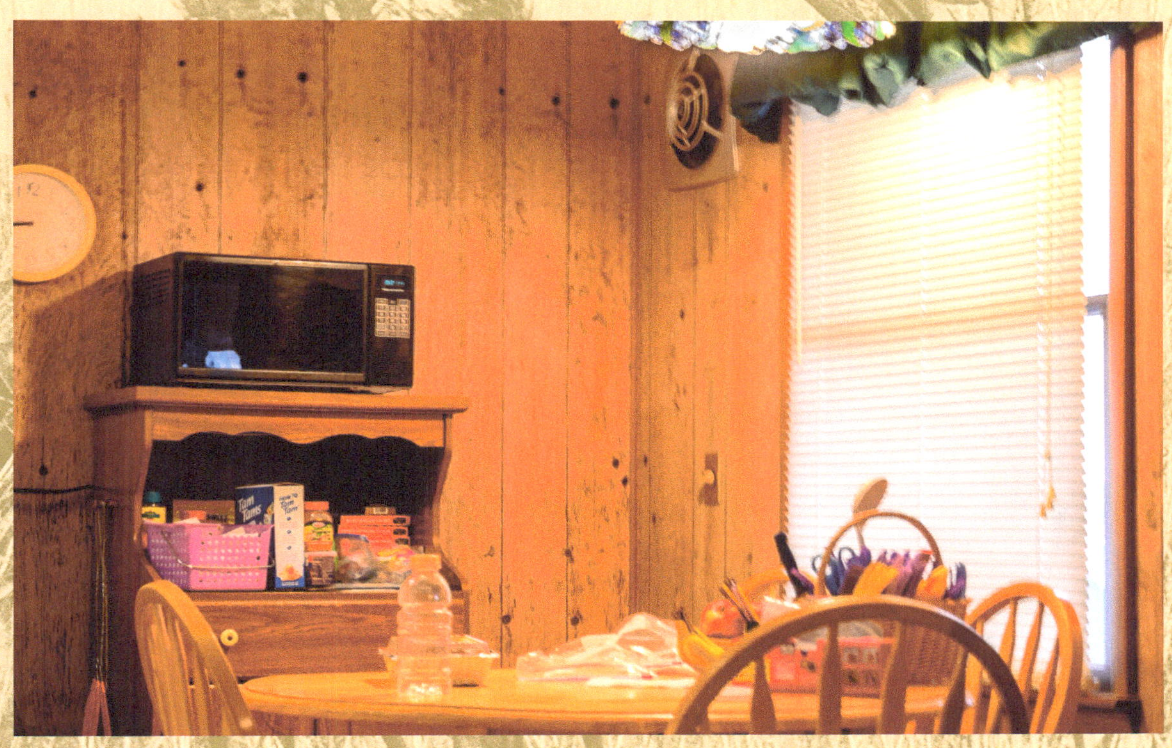

After the sun comes up over Assateague Channel, it's time for breakfast.

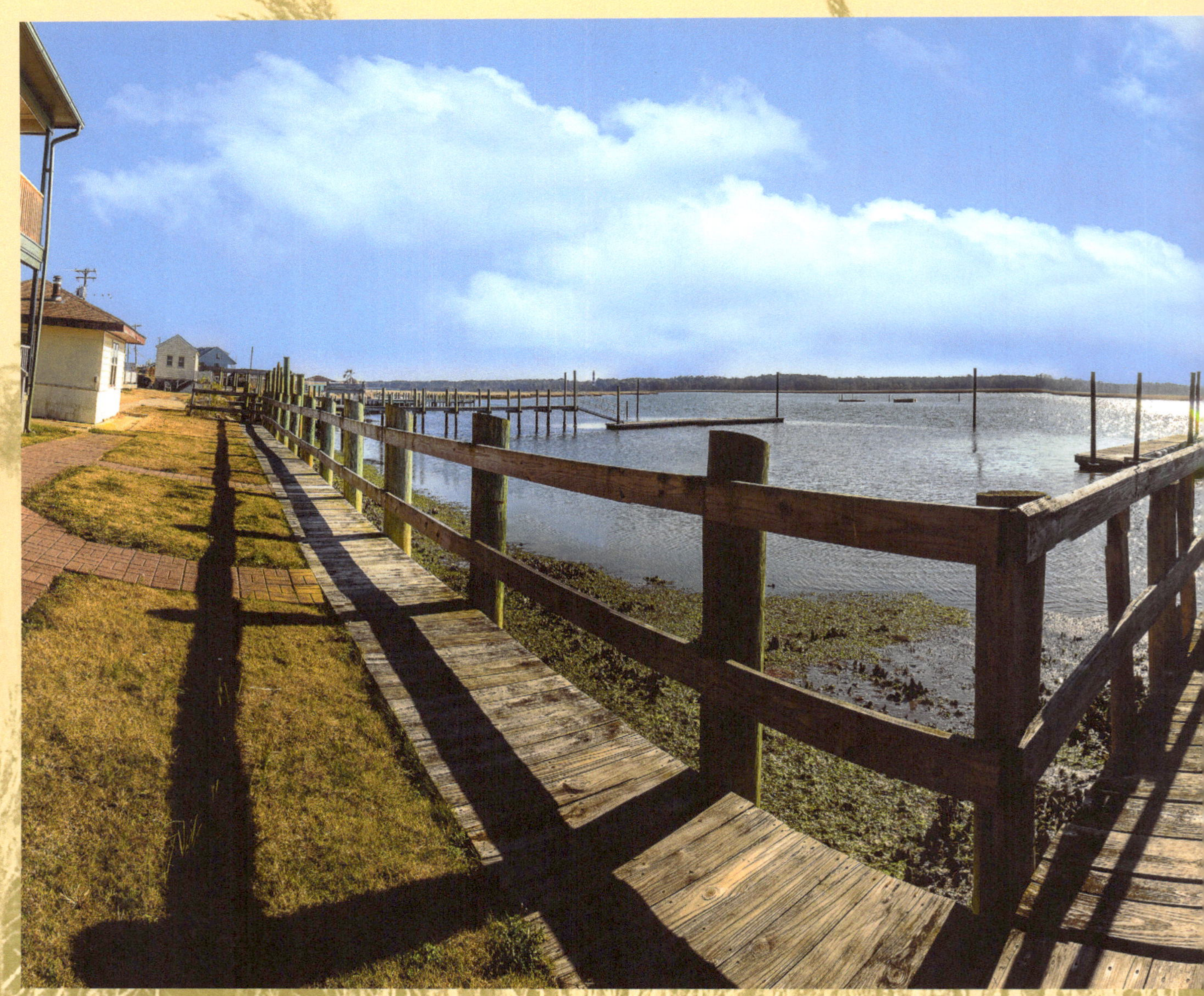

Rather than a back door, there are actually two front doors to our cottage: one facing the road (for landlubbers, like me, in cars), and one facing Assateague Channel (for mariners in boats). Here's a view of the channel.

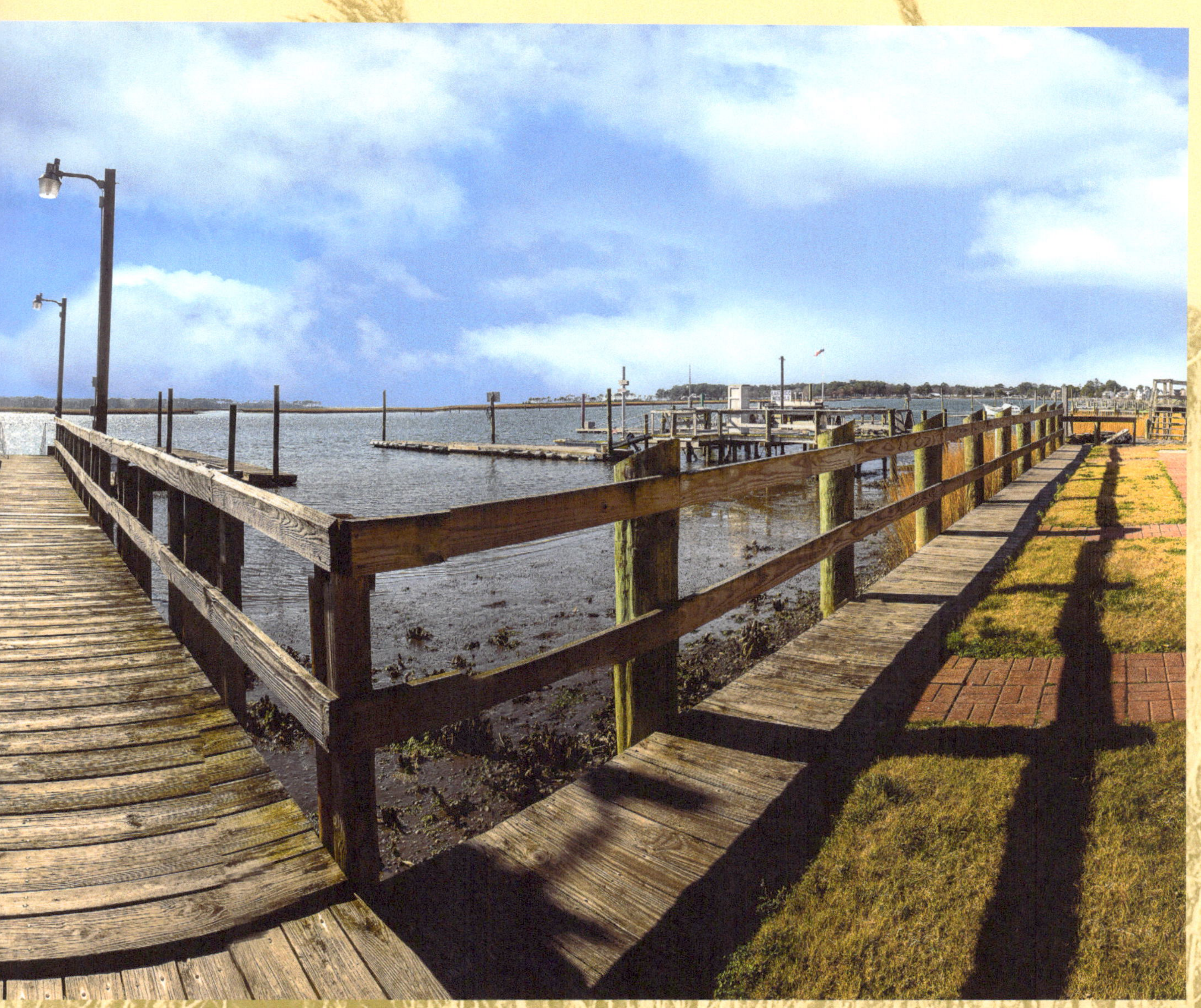

This is the pier outside our back door. Oops! I mean the other front door, of course. It shows how nice a morning anyone can enjoy on Chincoteague Island. And this is how nice it usually is, in any season.

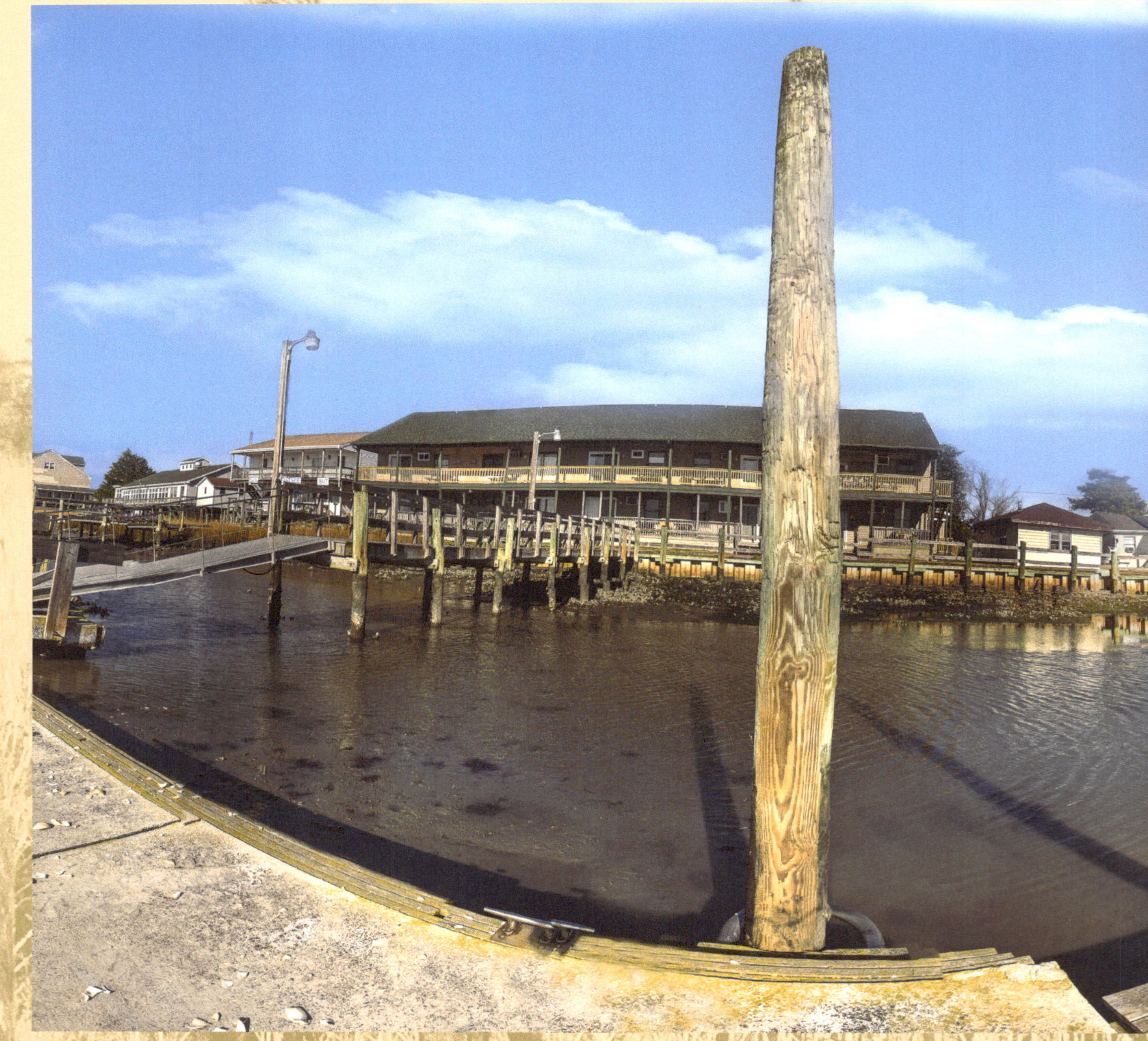

This is the view looking from the pier back at the cottages and other buildings onshore. The large building on the left is the one that included our cottage.

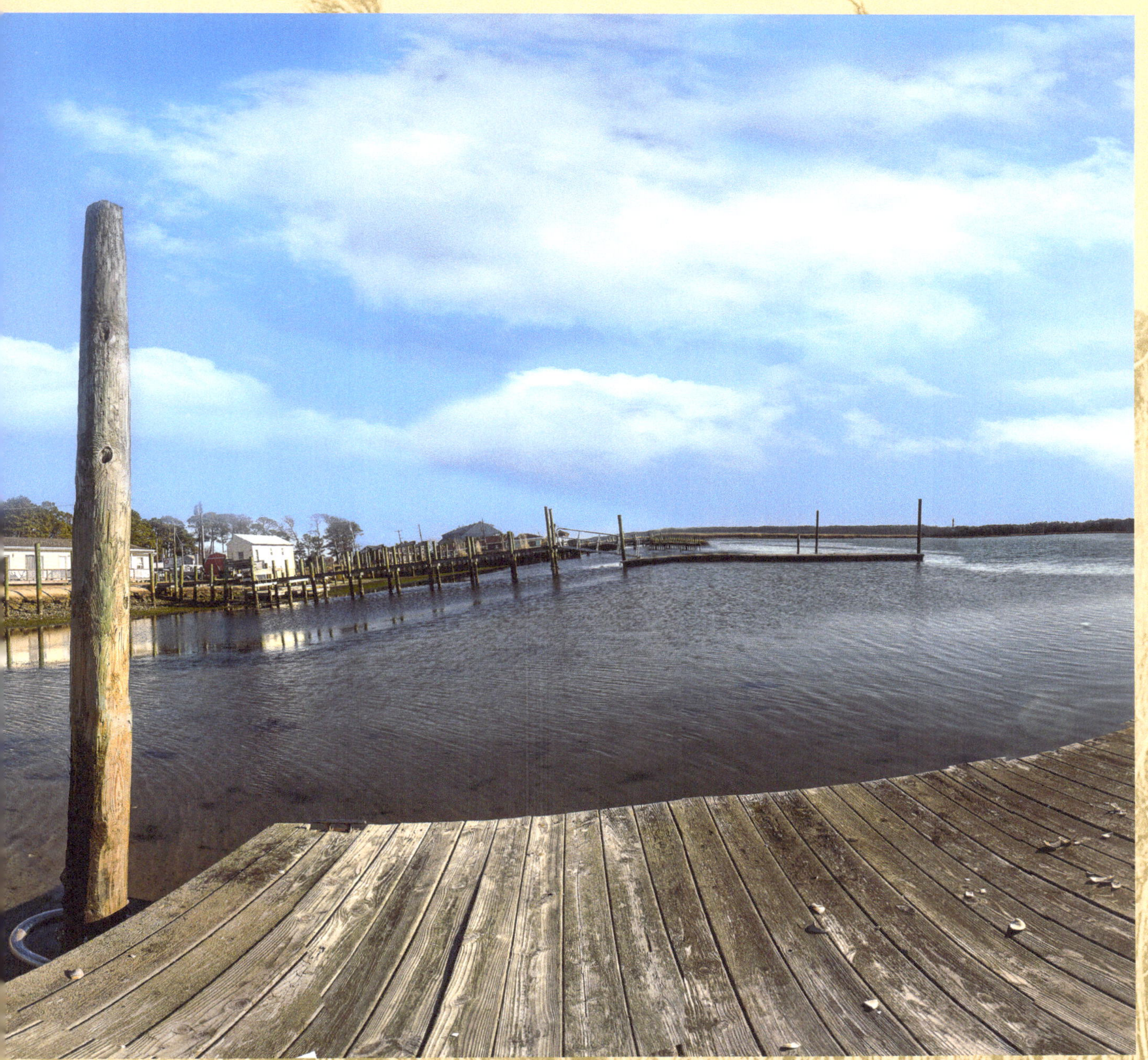

It's quiet here. Lovely! Just the way we like it.

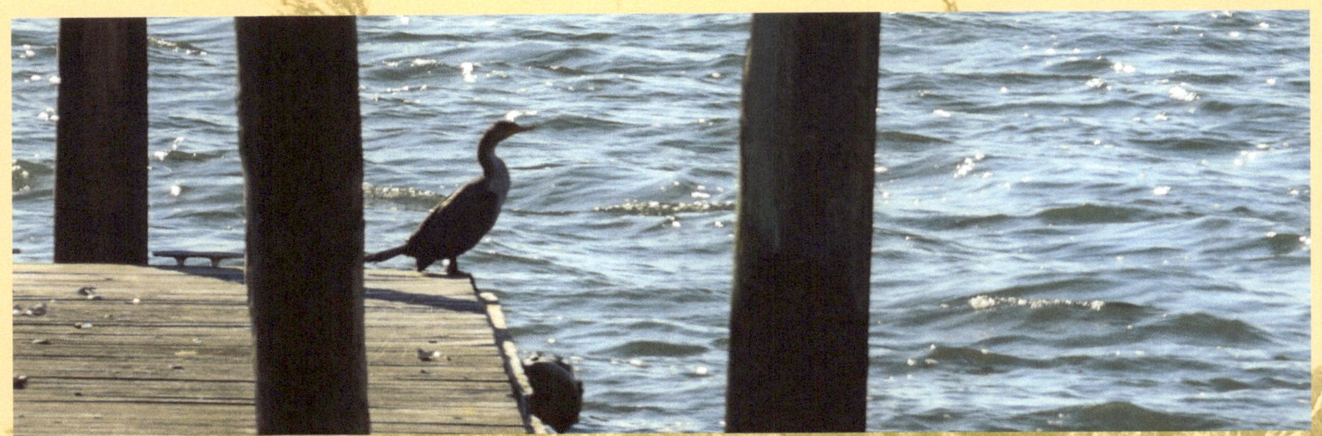

There are birds everywhere, especially near the water and on the piers on Chincoteague Island. Here, a double-crested cormorant is warming in the morning sun.

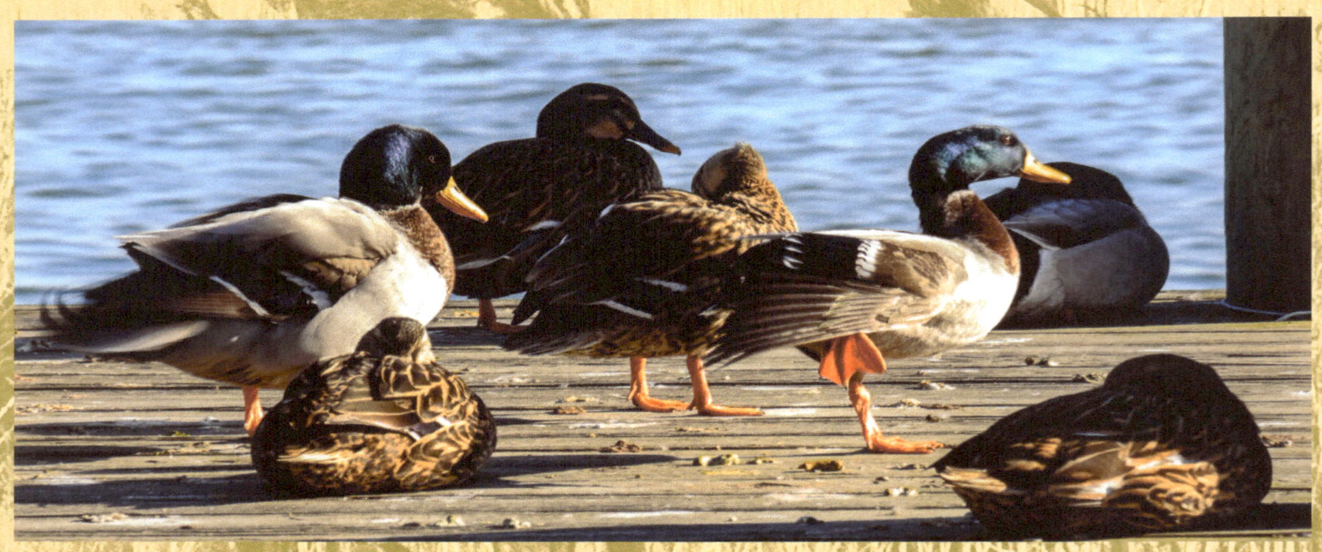

These mallard ducks are enjoying a pier too. Ducks, of course, really take to water.

Chincoteague & Assateague

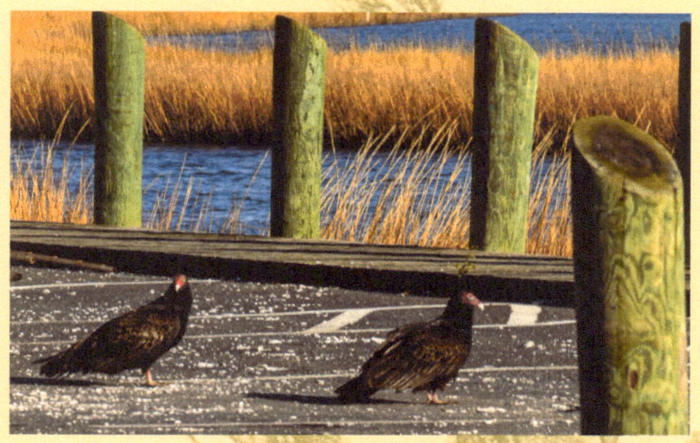

These turkey vultures are digesting a good meal ...

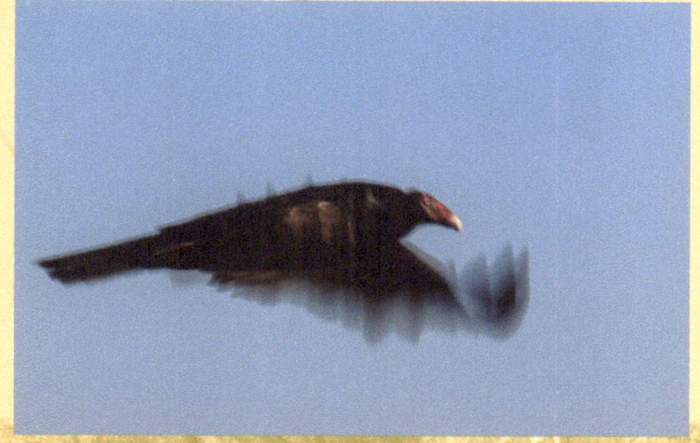

... but this one is still looking around.

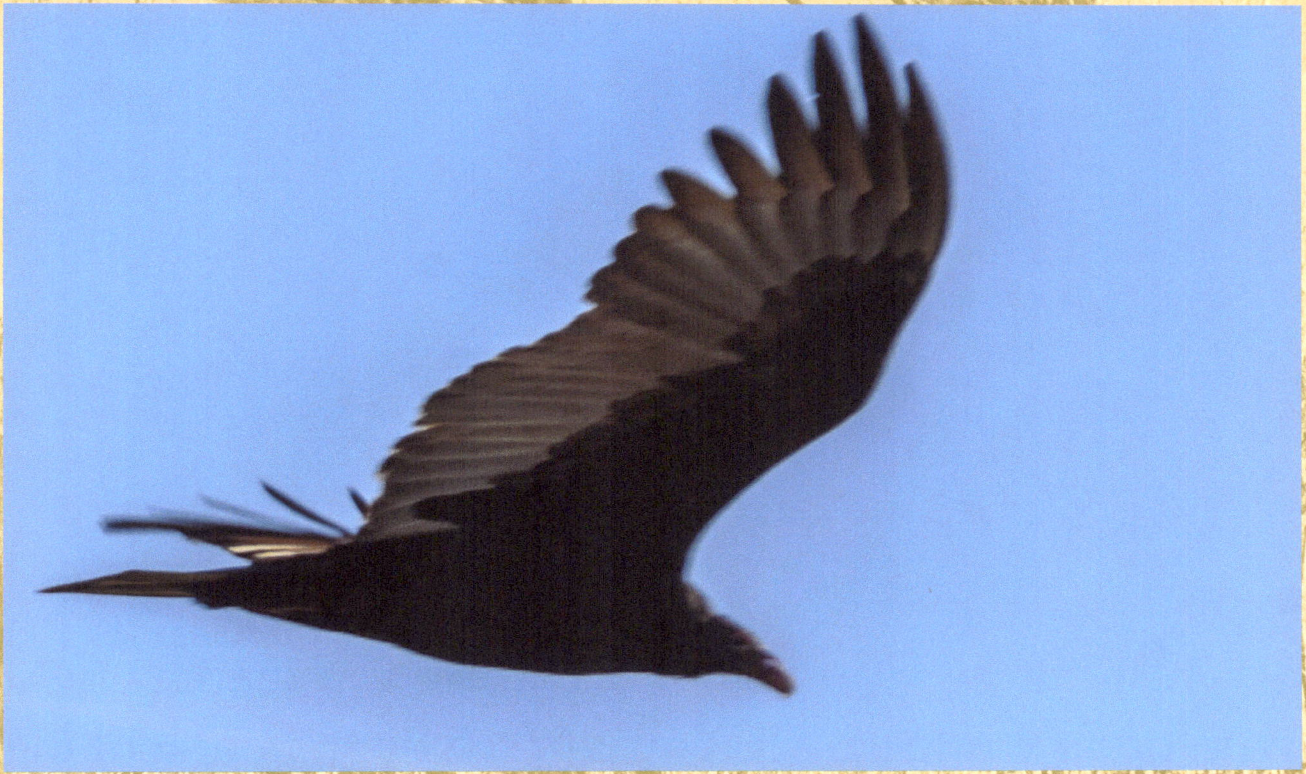

This black vulture stays close to the turkey vultures, because he knows they have much keener noses for that yummy rotten food.

Discovering Chincoteague Island

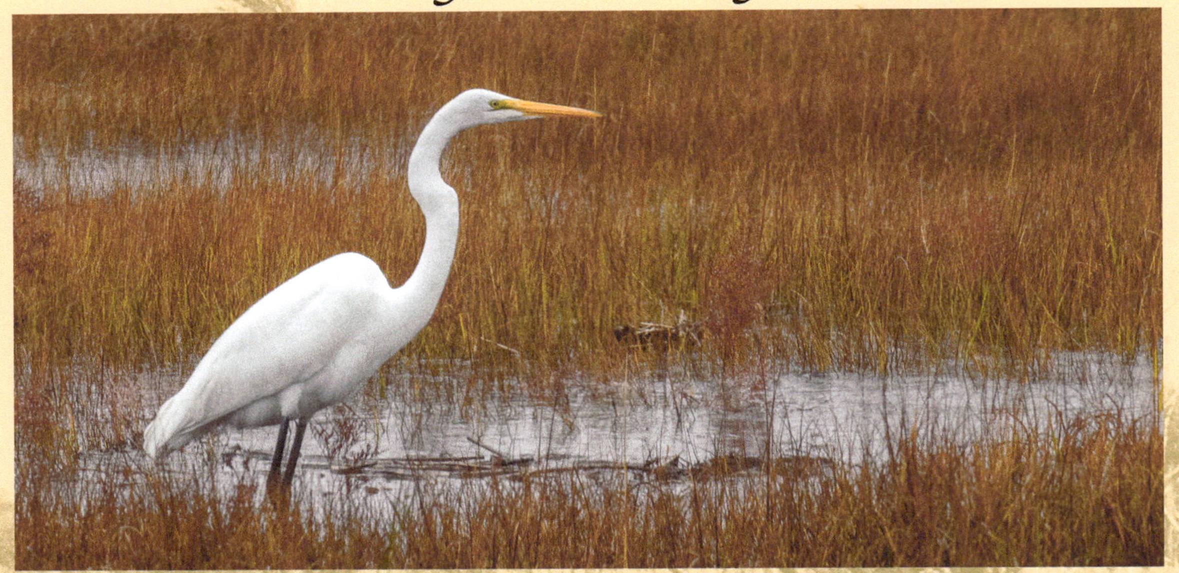

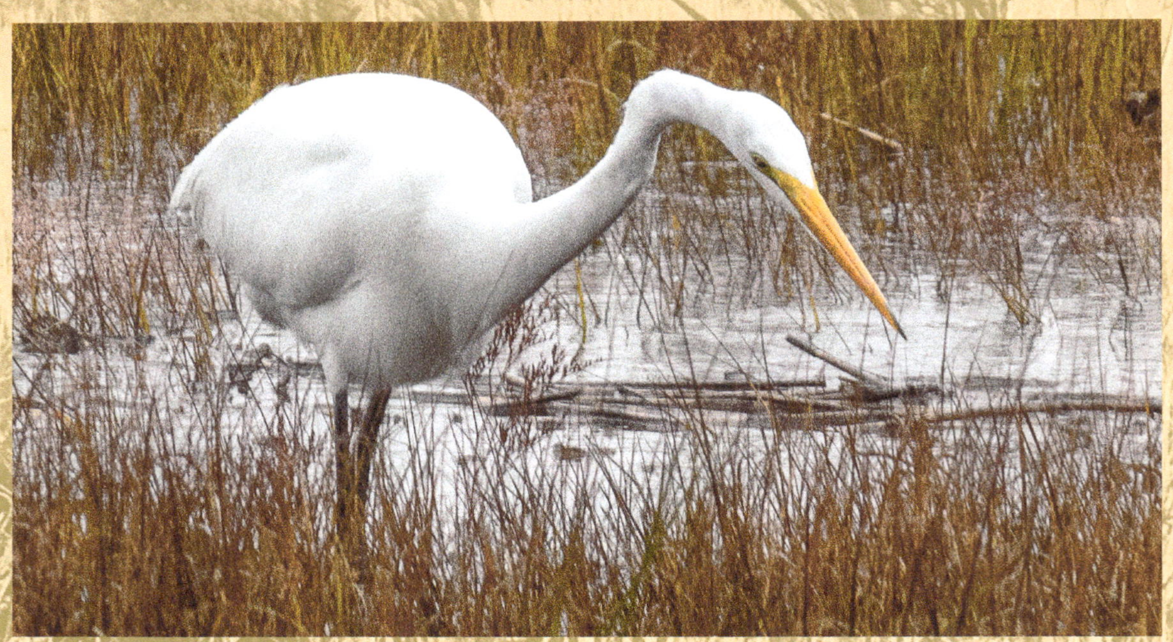

Just off the road near our cottage is a marshy field with great white egrets. You can see them here looking for a tasty snack—you fish and frogs had better watch out.

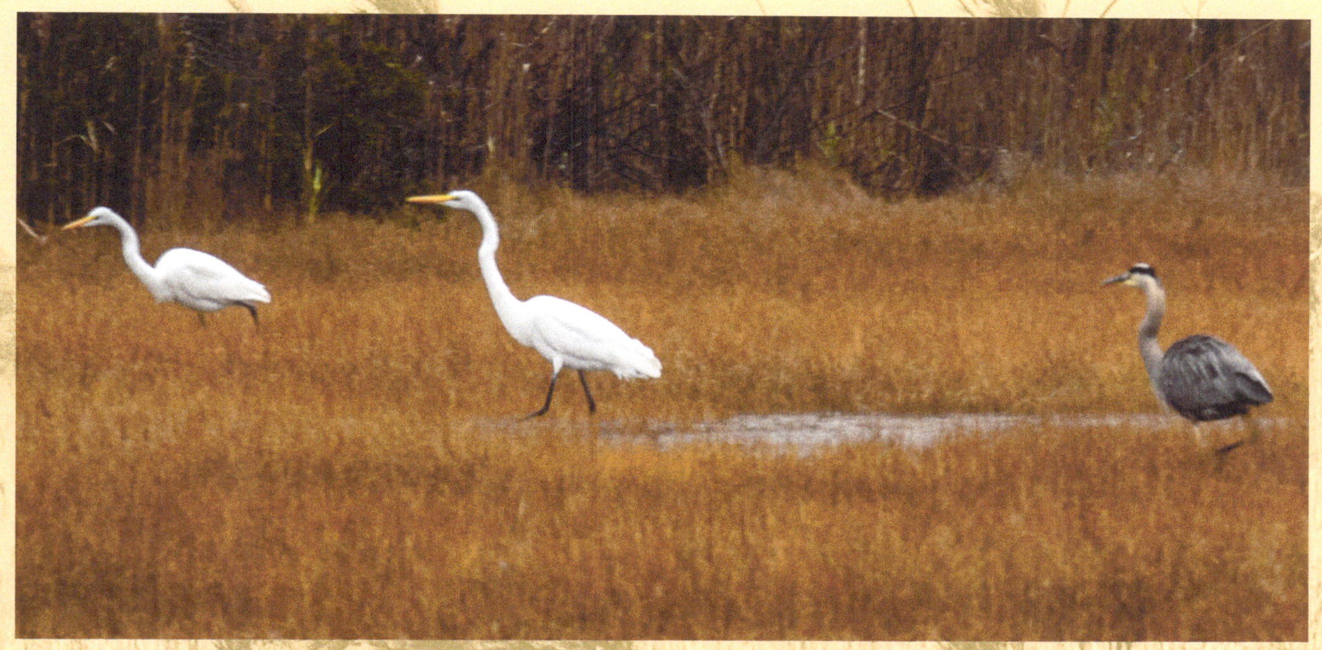

    This great blue heron knows that egrets have a similar taste in food, and he shadows his cousins, looking for hints on where to find the goodies. Egrets and herons are closely related genetically.

    It sure looks wet, huh? But these birds seem to like it that way.

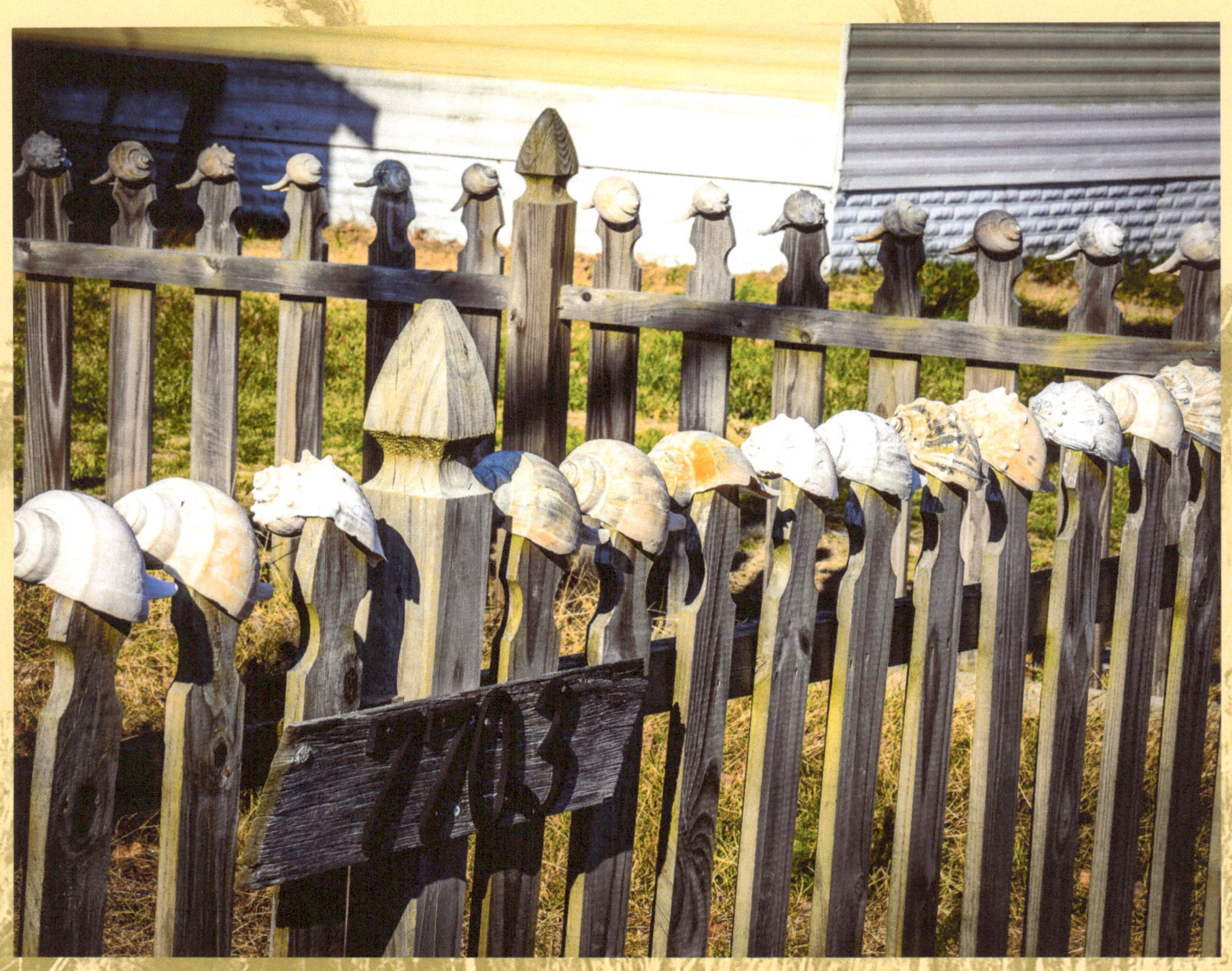

Of course there are also people in the quiet rural town of Chincoteague who love everything about the sea, and who take advantage of the gifts of the sea.

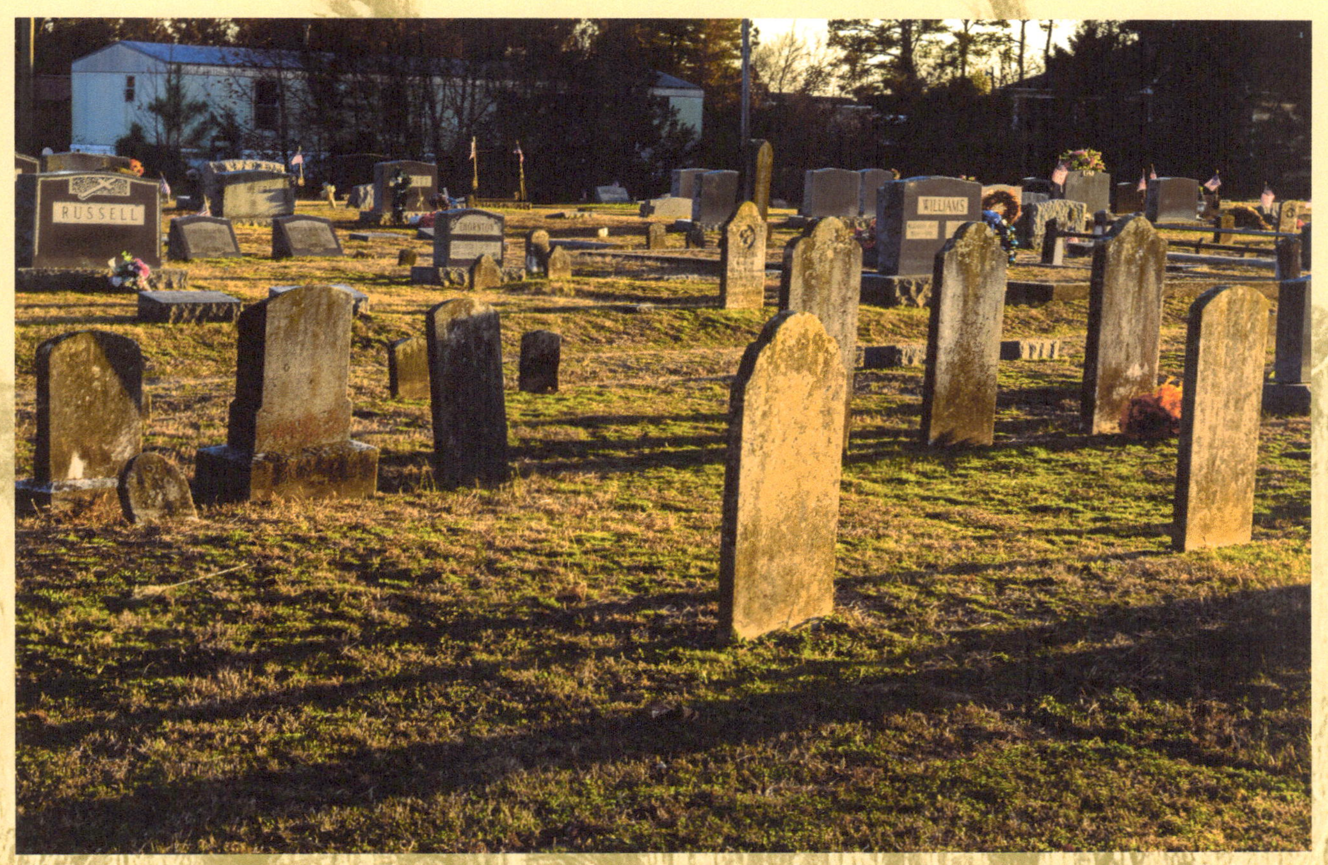

And here the living make room for the dead, and lovingly celebrate their memory.

After all this adventure, we drive over to Sundial Books on Main Street for a rich literary buffet, and then over to Maria's Restaurant on Maddox Boulevard for a lovely gustatory buffet.

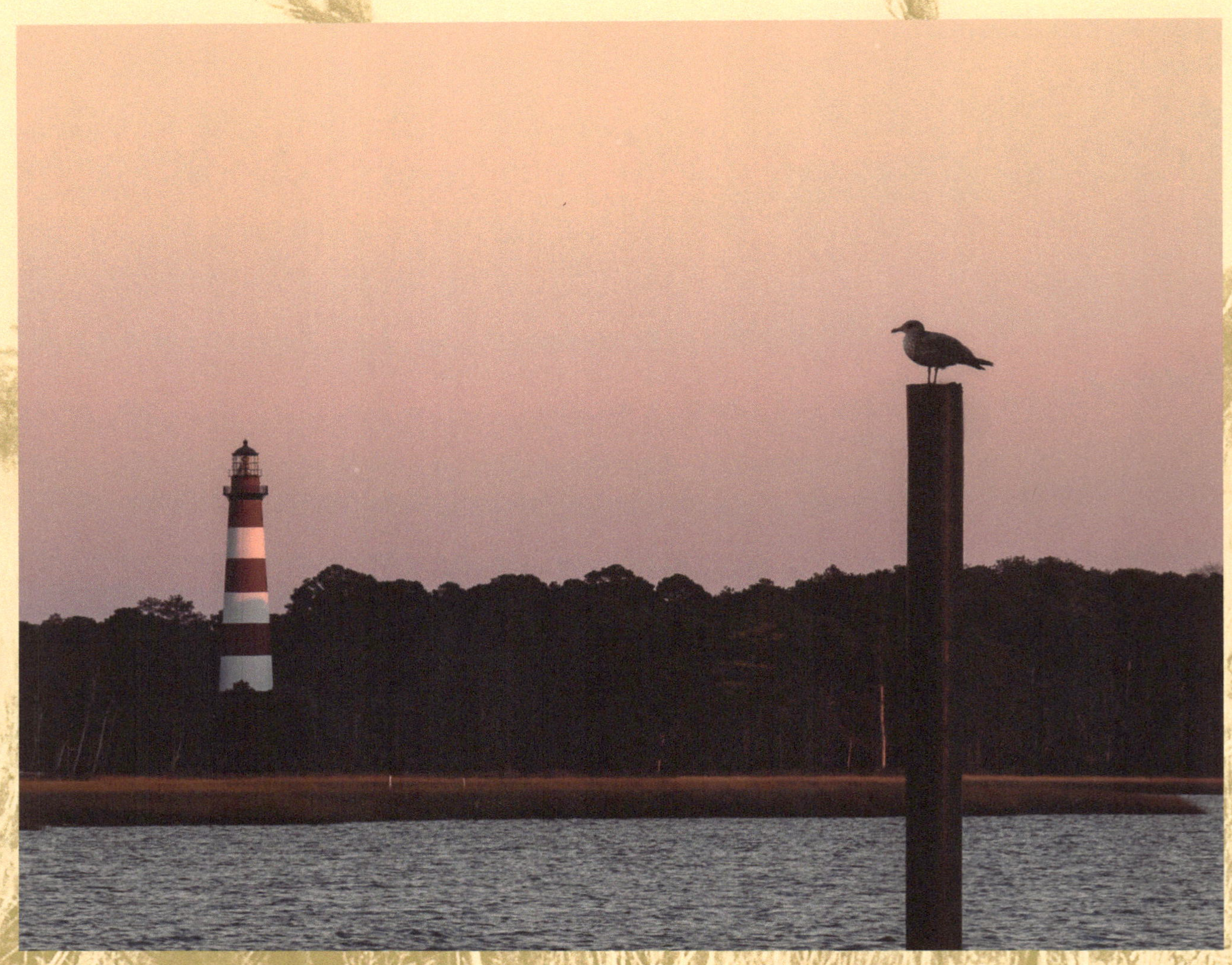

Back at the cottage on Chincoteague Island, at the end of a very birdy day, we, and all the birds too, start to unwind. This bird is enjoying a relaxing setting.

Chincoteague & Assateague

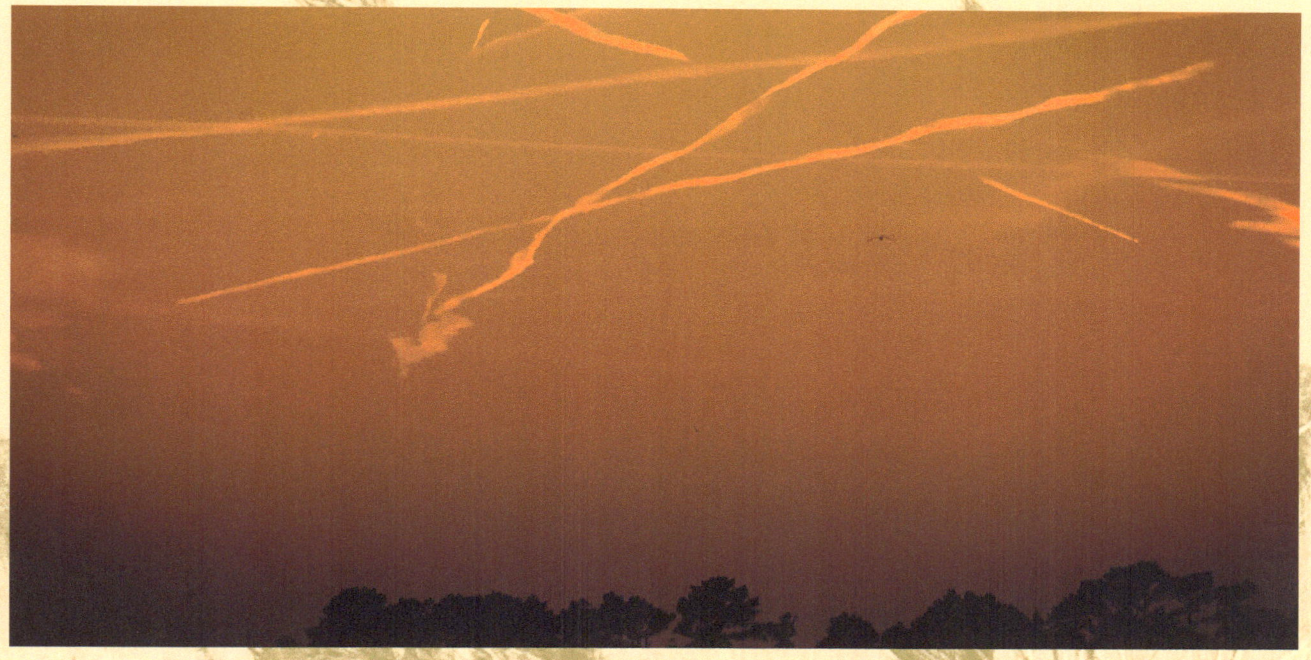

Vapor trails criss-cross the evening sky, probably from the Wallops Island rocket launching facility of NASA, south of Chincoteague Island.

The neighborhood to the south is quiet as usual.

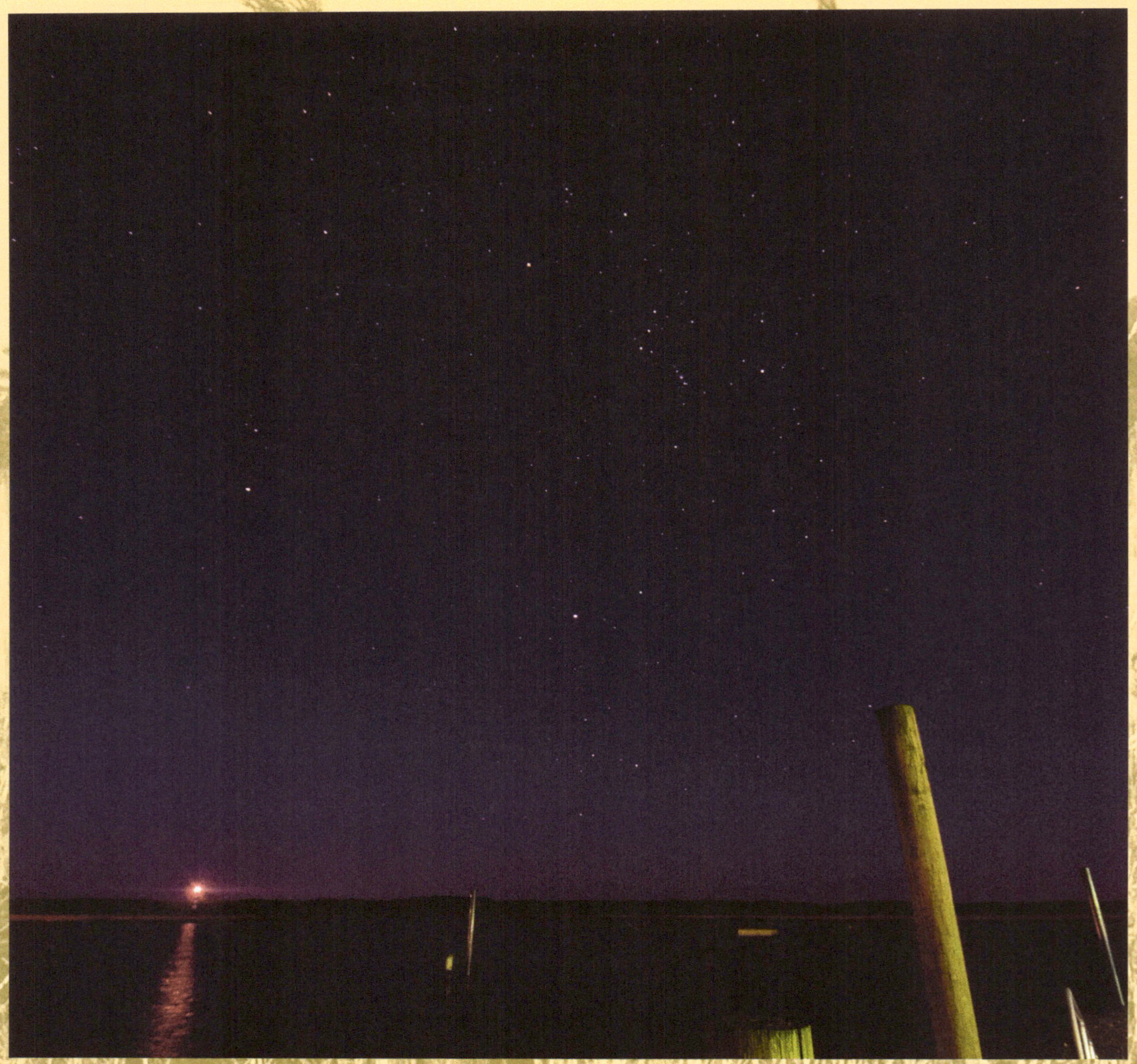

Chincoteague Island has a great night sky. Here is the starry, starry sky, brilliant to the east, punctuated by the lighthouse seen across Assateague Channel.

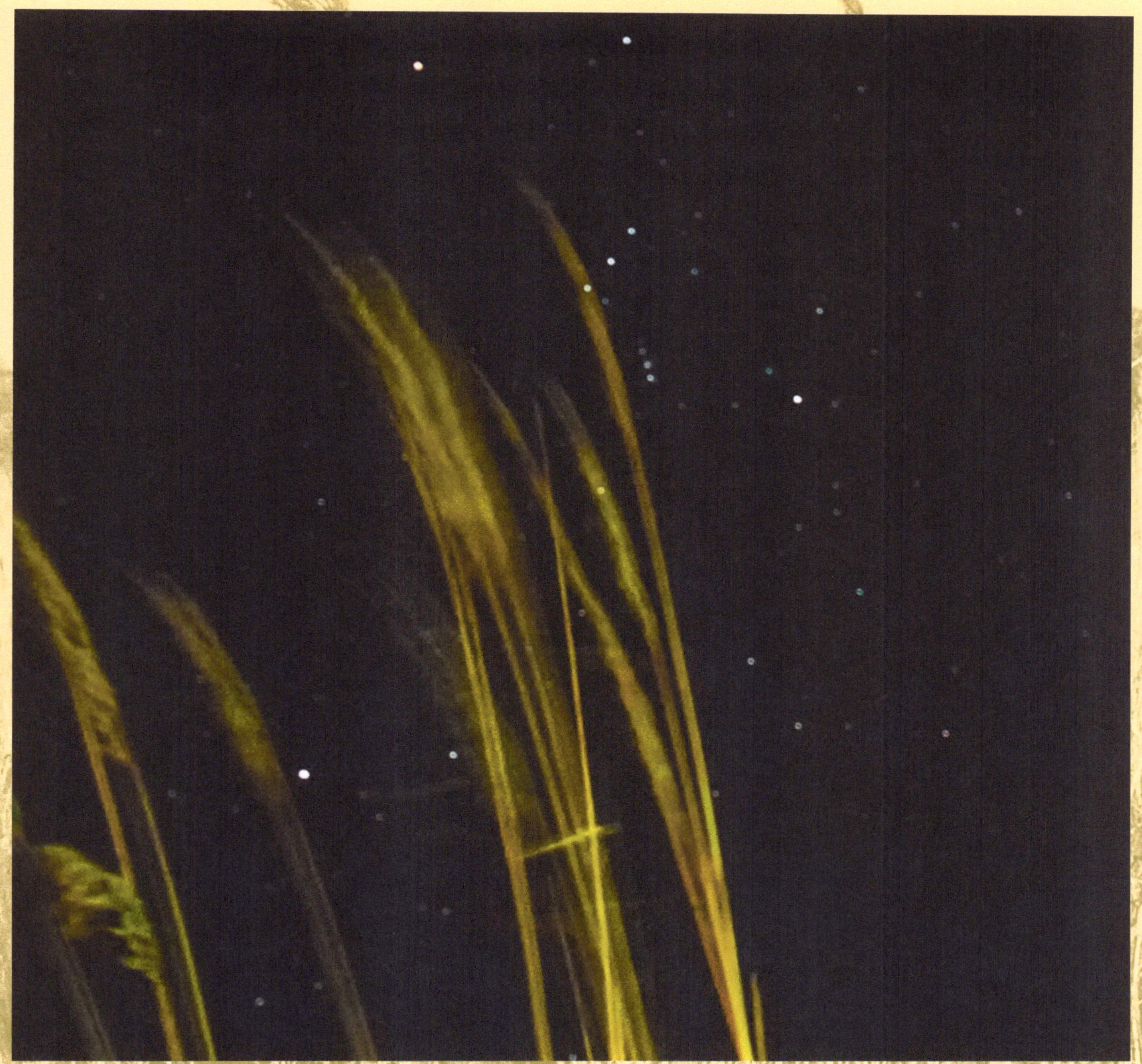

The constellation Orion shows through this clump of dune grass. Is Orion the Hunter looking for birds? What do you think?

To the south, the sky features a light scattering of clouds, with the moon peeking through, reflecting in the waters of the Assateague Channel

and illuminating the marsh grass. Piers far to the south show a variety of colored lights.

Chapter 3 --
An Exploration
of Nature

Red sky in the morning, sailors take warning!

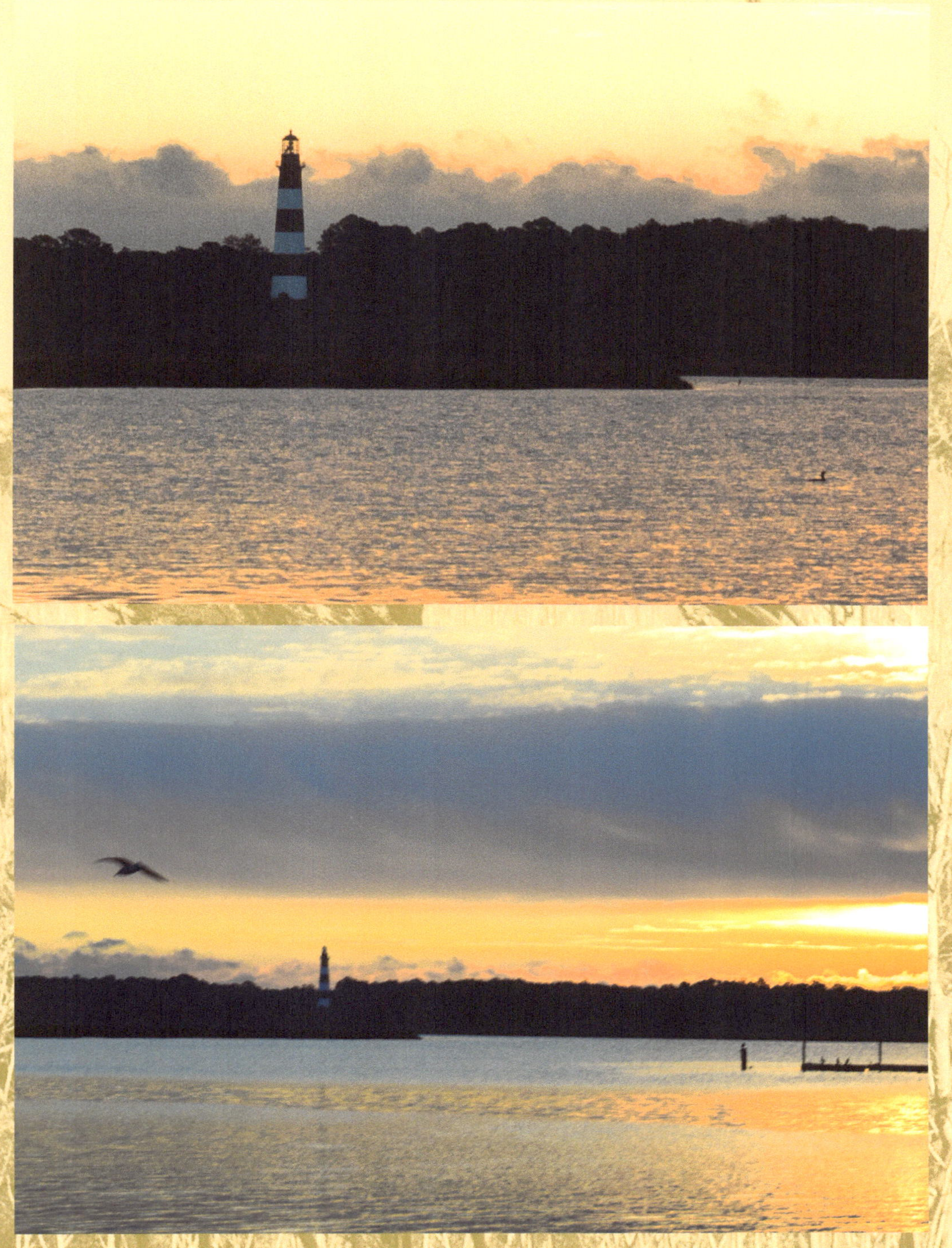

But the early birds don't seem worried at all. They're just too busy for that kind of nonsense.

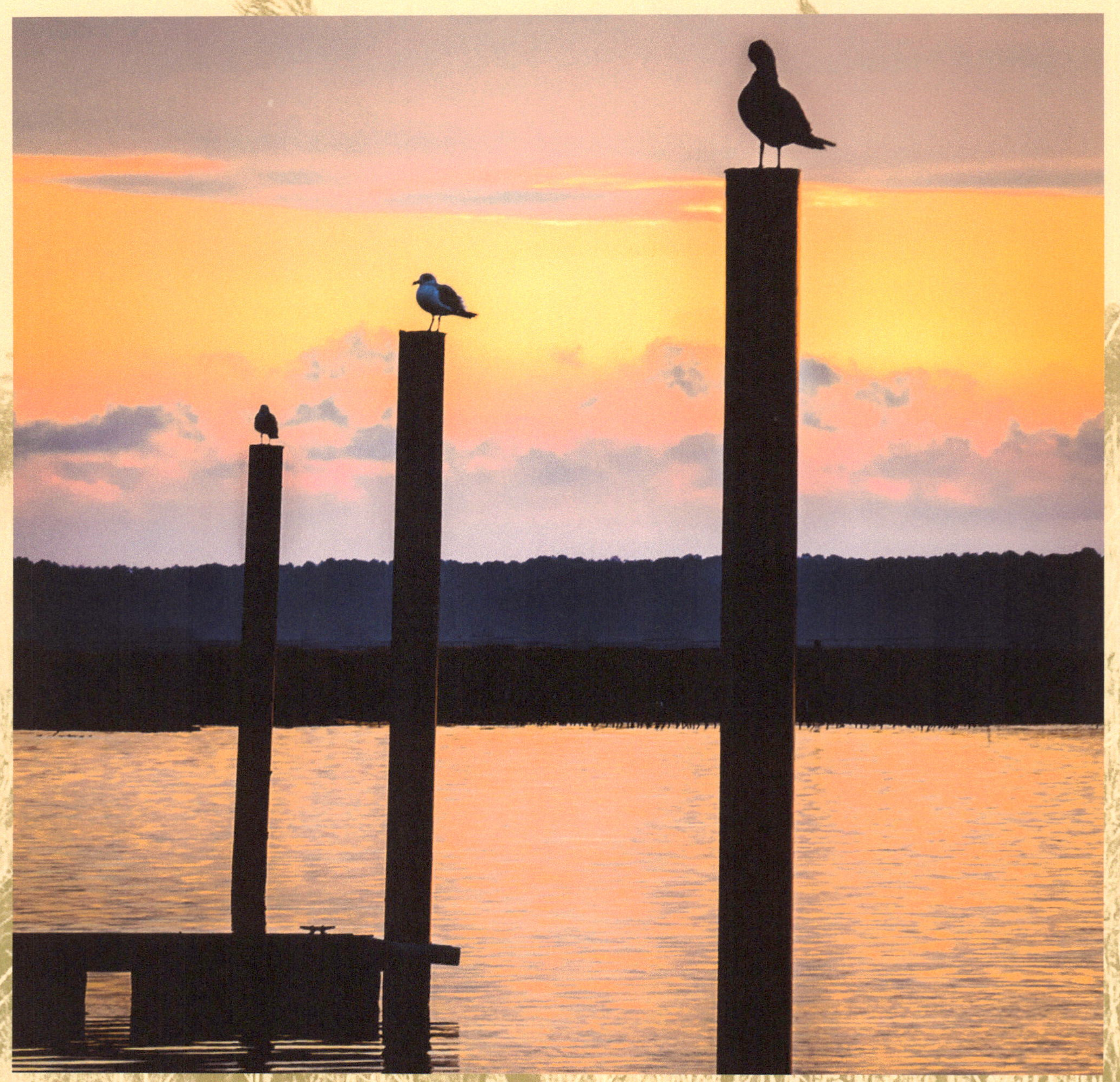

Some gulls and a duck (rightmost bird) enjoy the calm of the morning ...

Chincoteague & Assateague

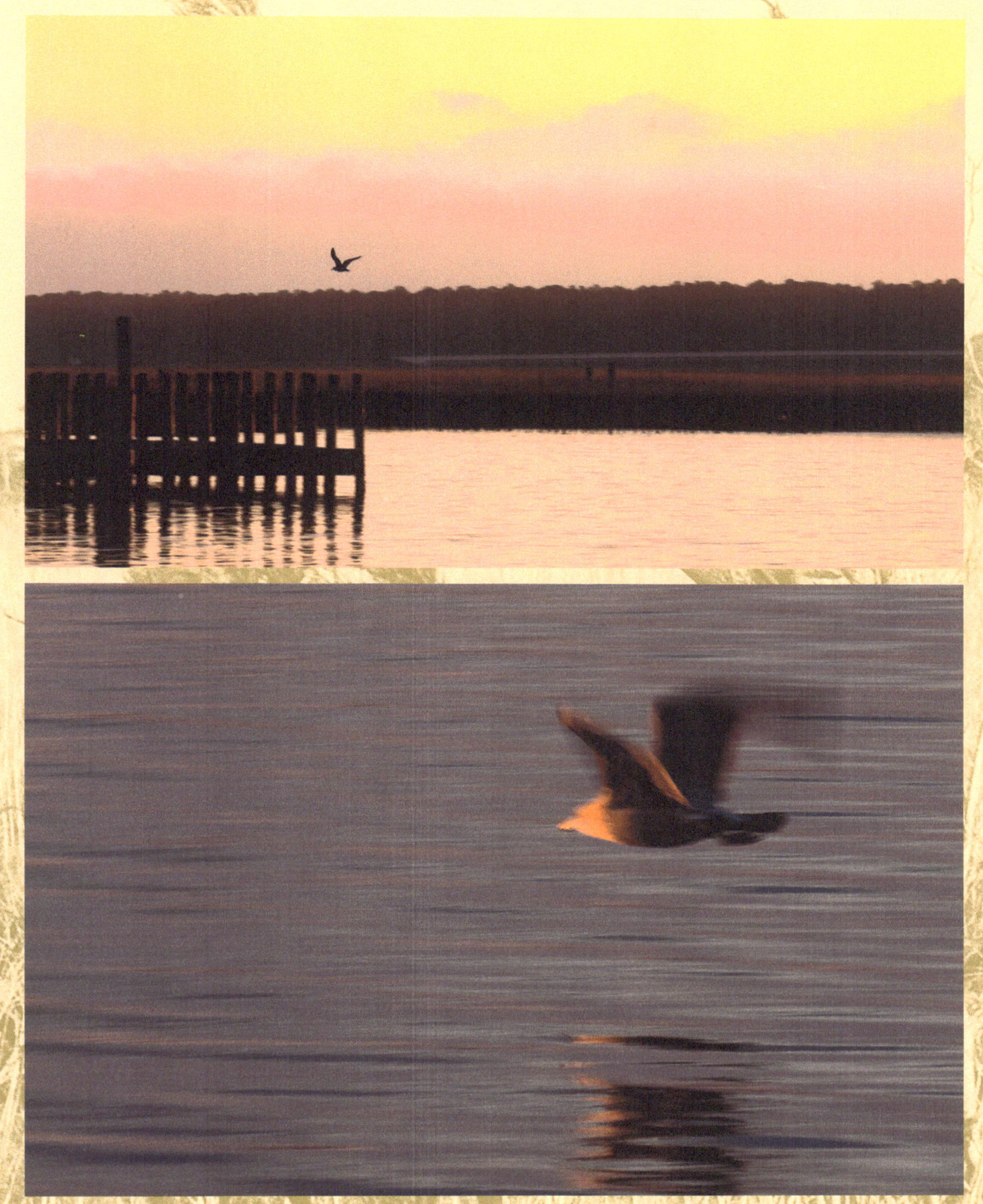

... while others have places to go and things to do.

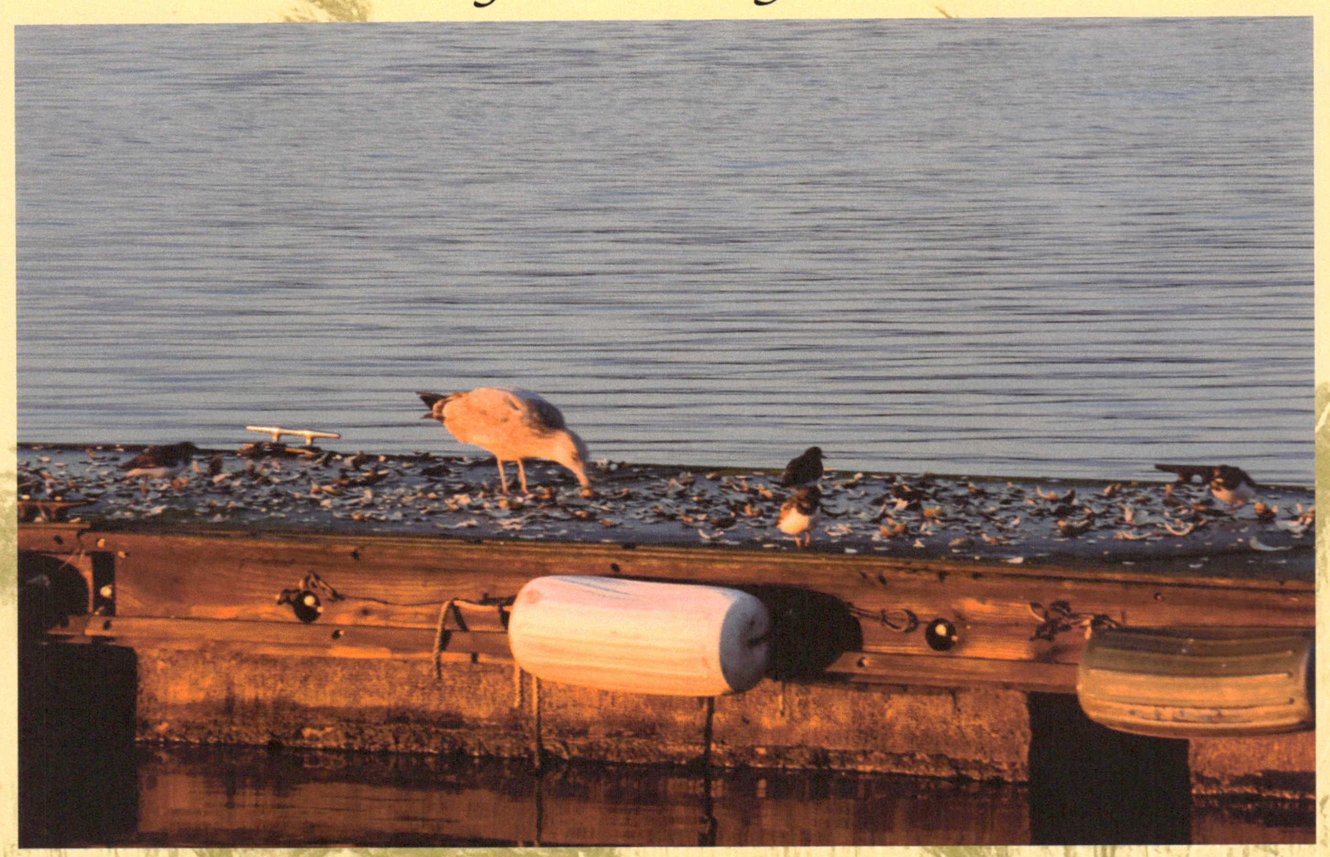

Hungry gulls are grabbing clams and dropping them on the pier to crack them open. This herring gull is nice enough to share its bounty with other hungry birds, such as these ruddy turnstones.

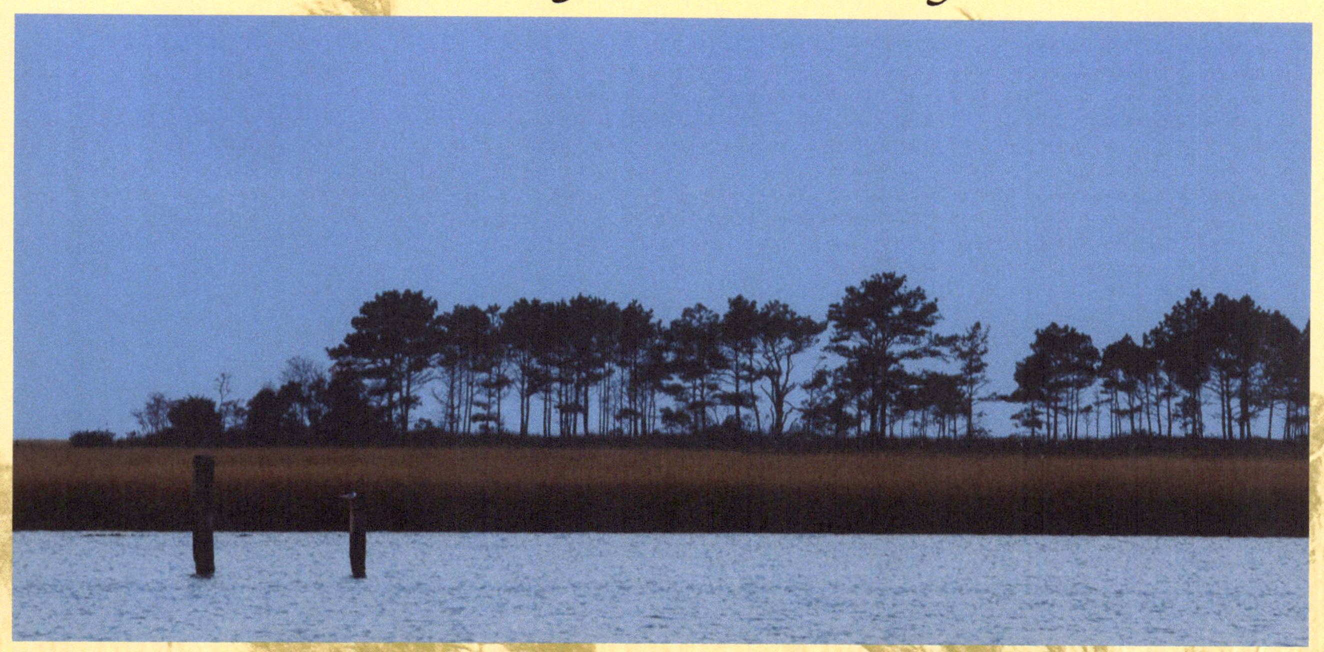

Resiliant loblolly pines grace the shores to the south.

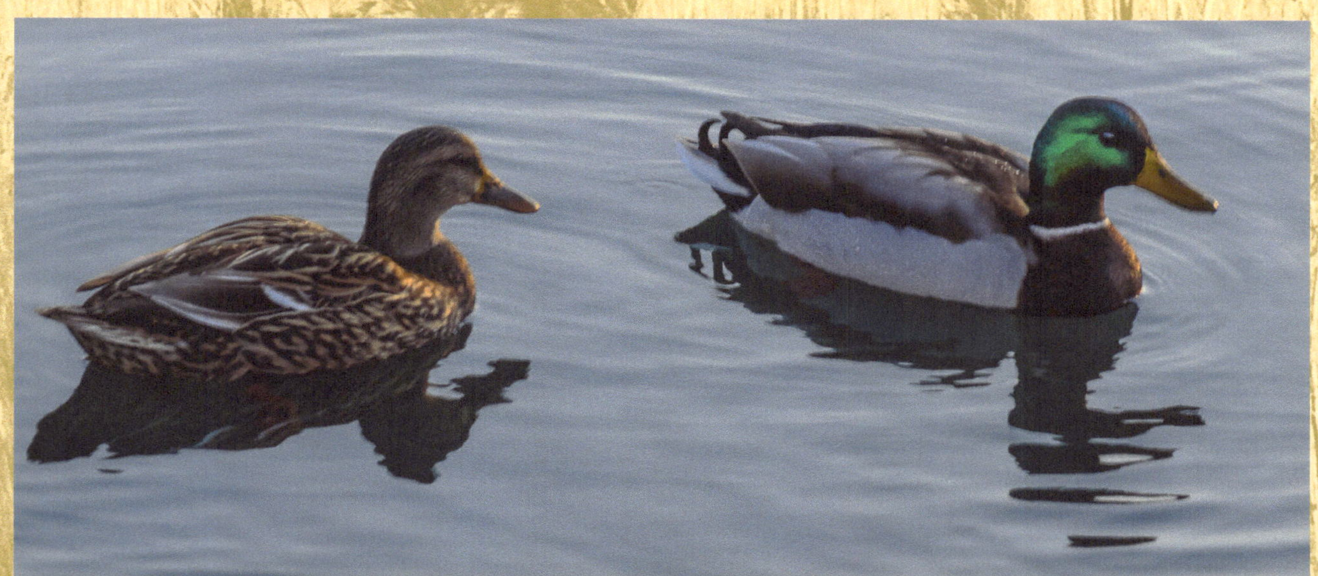

And a mallard duck couple are enjoying moments of loving closeness.

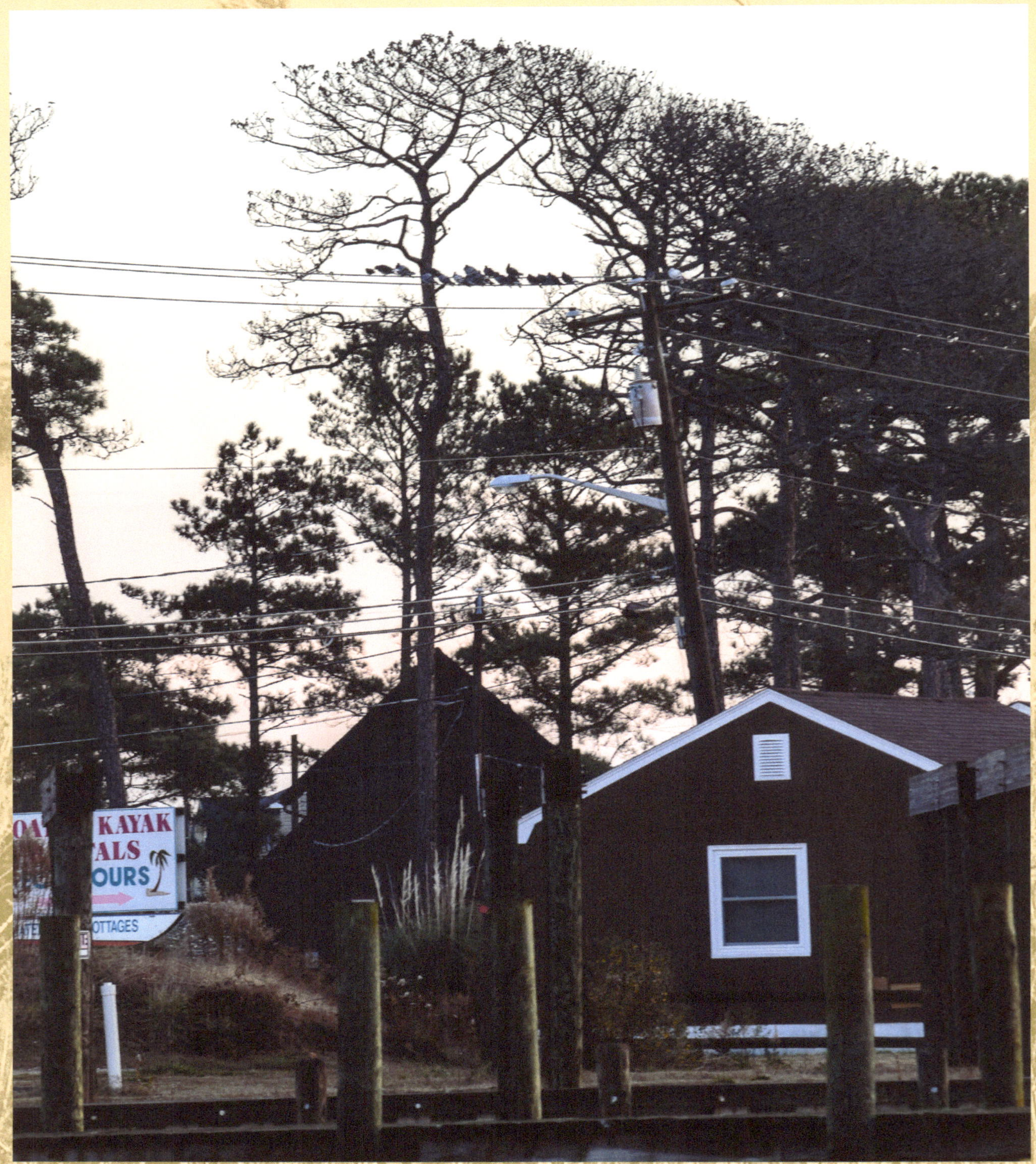

Doves roost on a wire next door.

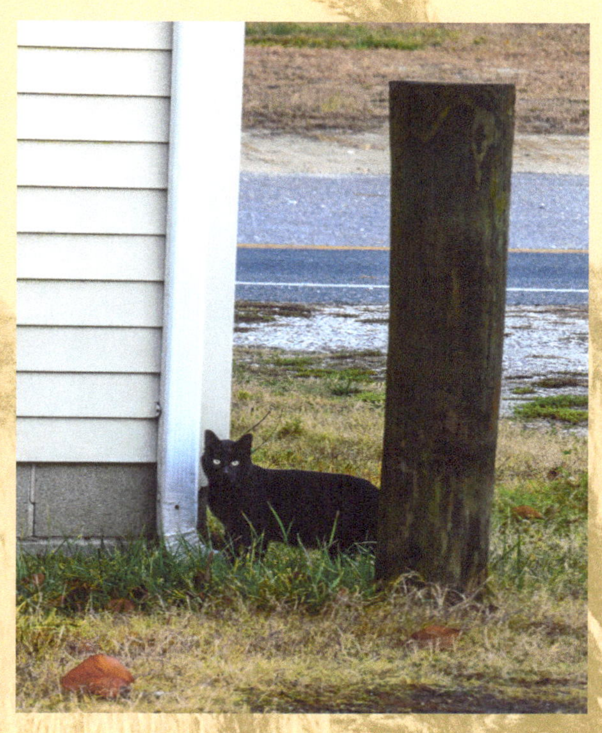

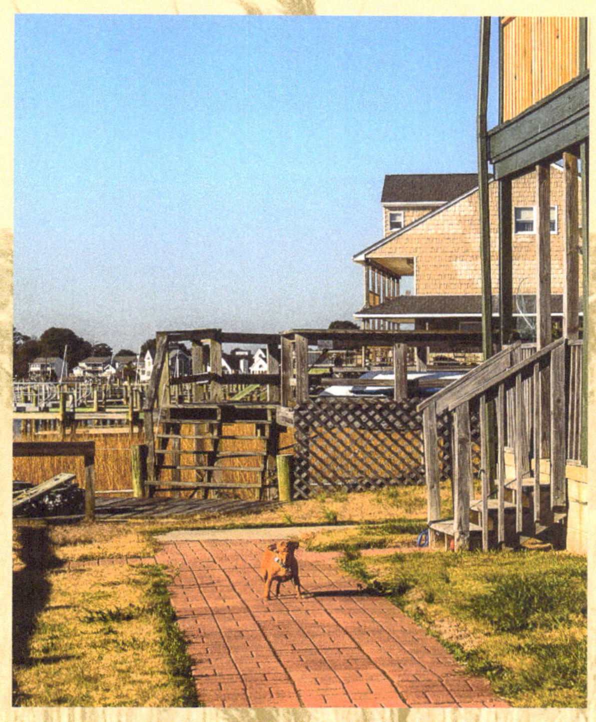

And other animals, decidedly more domestic, are lurking about ...

... or trying hard to get my attention.

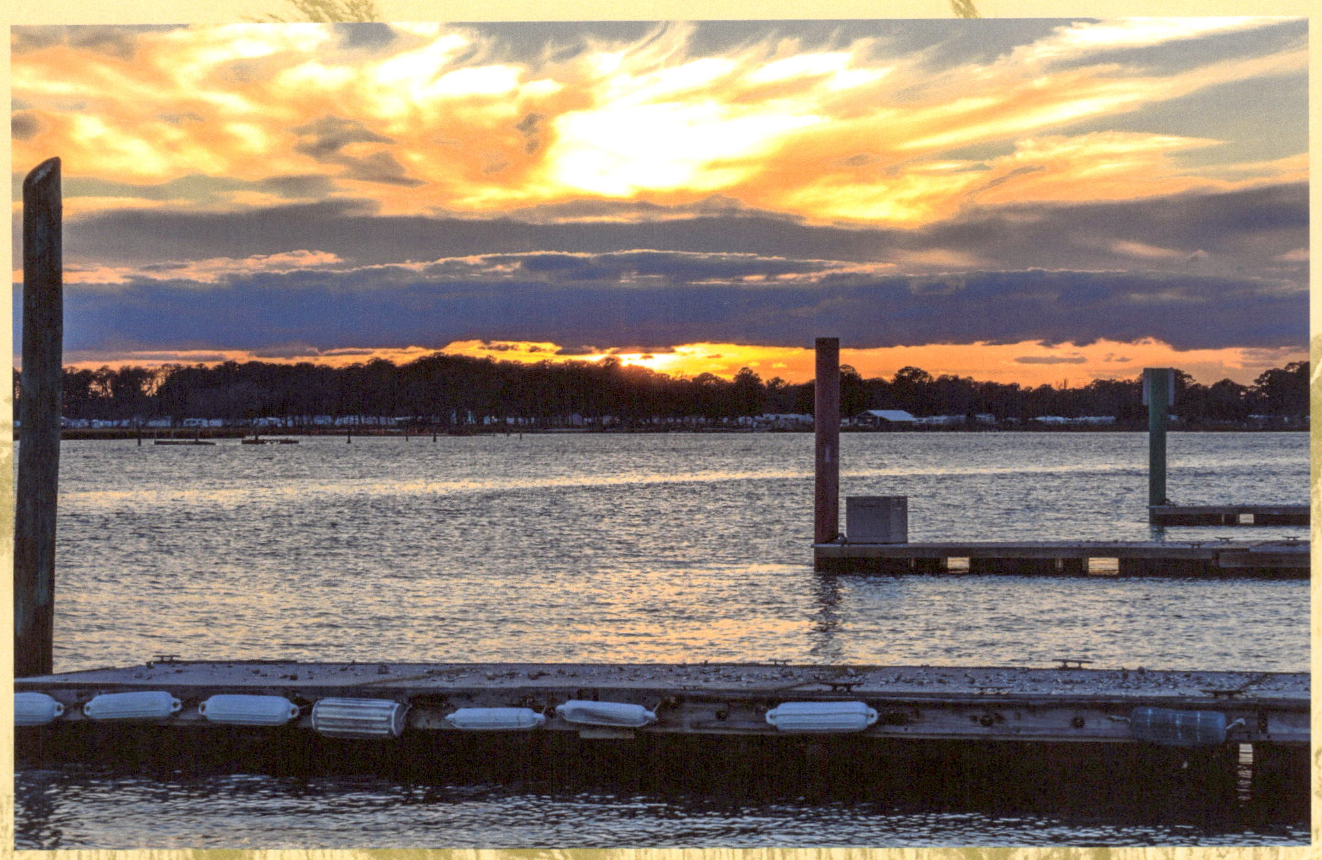

It's near the end of the day. Here is the view looking out the, dare this landlubber say, back door.

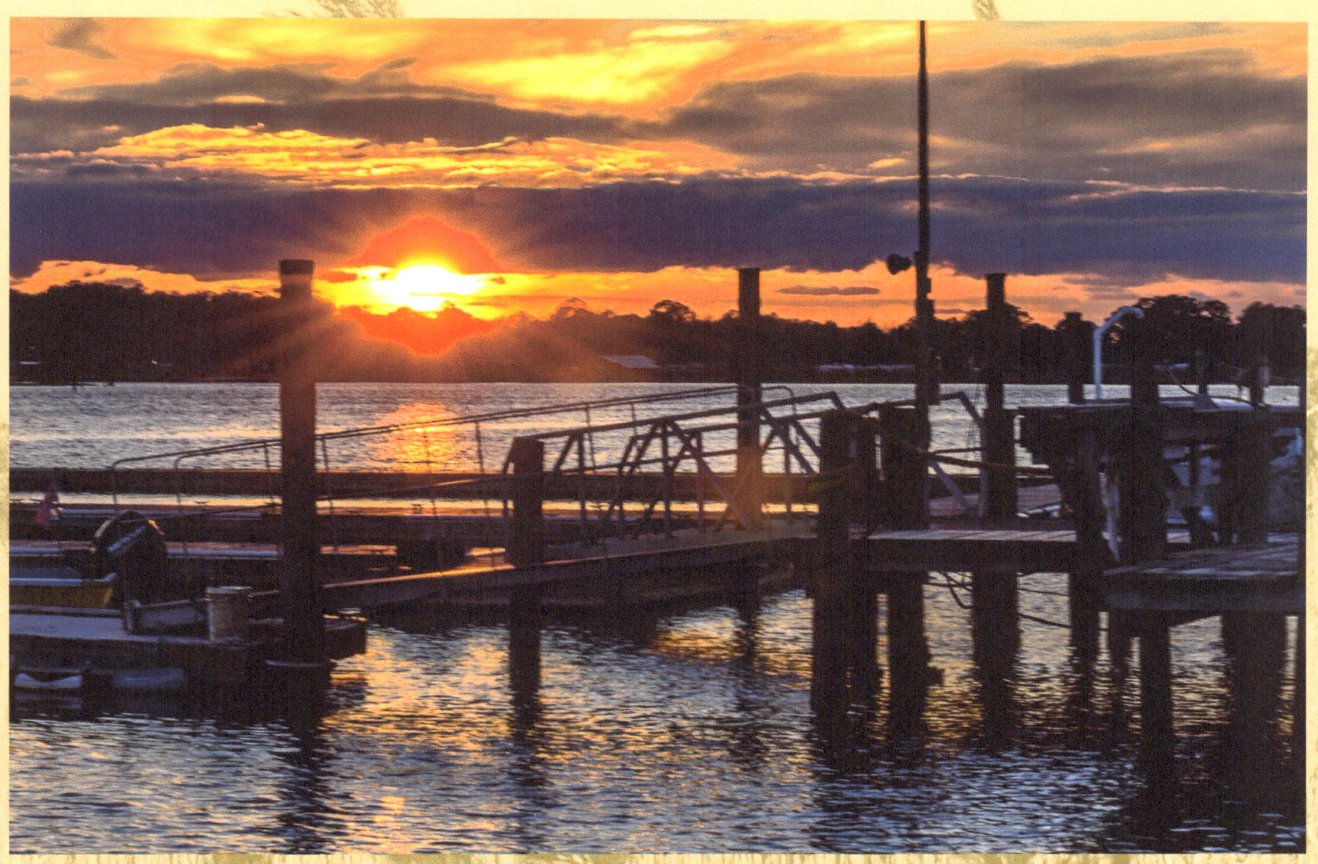

The sun is setting.

    Red sky at night, sailors' delight!
    And our delight too.

People can get tired after a long day of nature, so we duck inside to enjoy a secluded and restful evening.

Chapter 4 -- Visit the Lighthouse

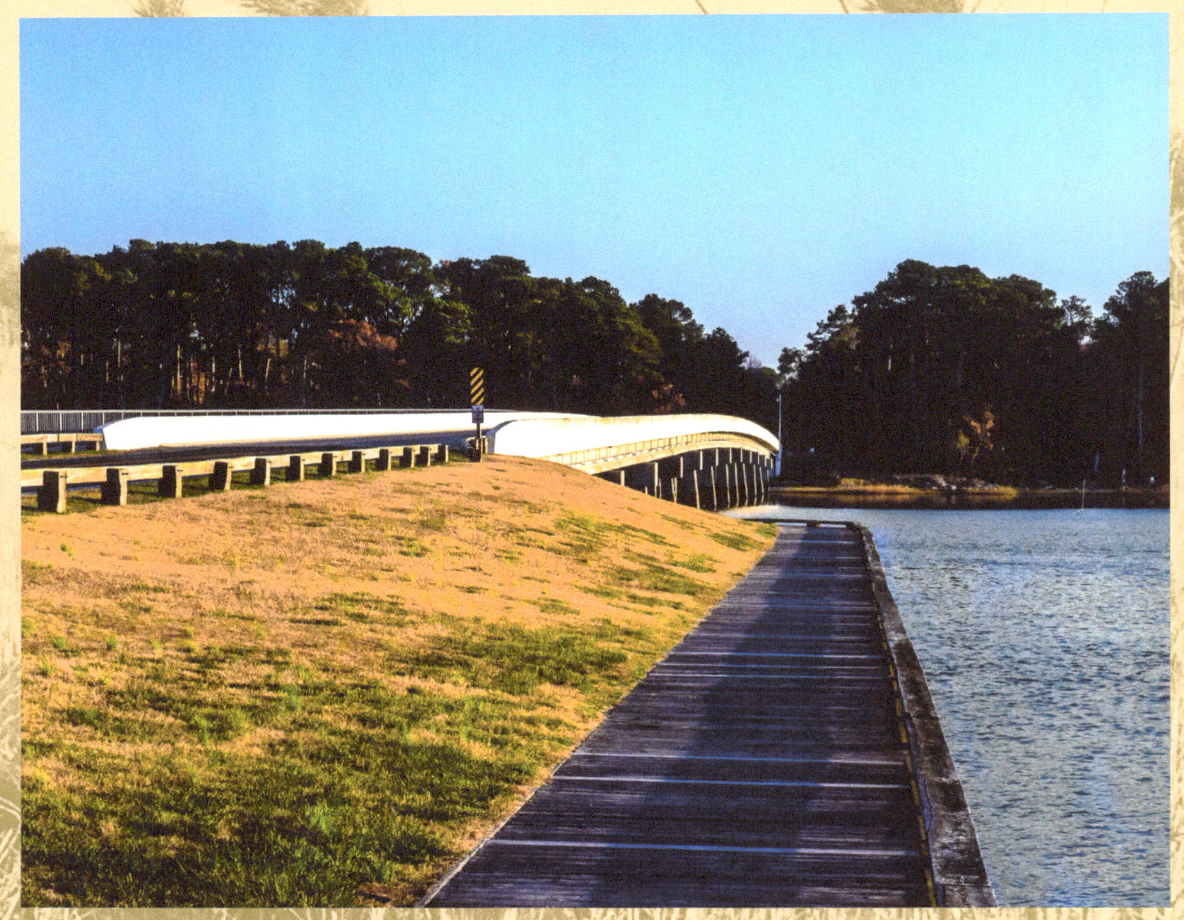

From so many locations you are tantalized by the view in the distance of the Assateague IslandLighthouse. So now we're crossing the bridge from Chincoteague Island to Assateague Island to actually see it up close.

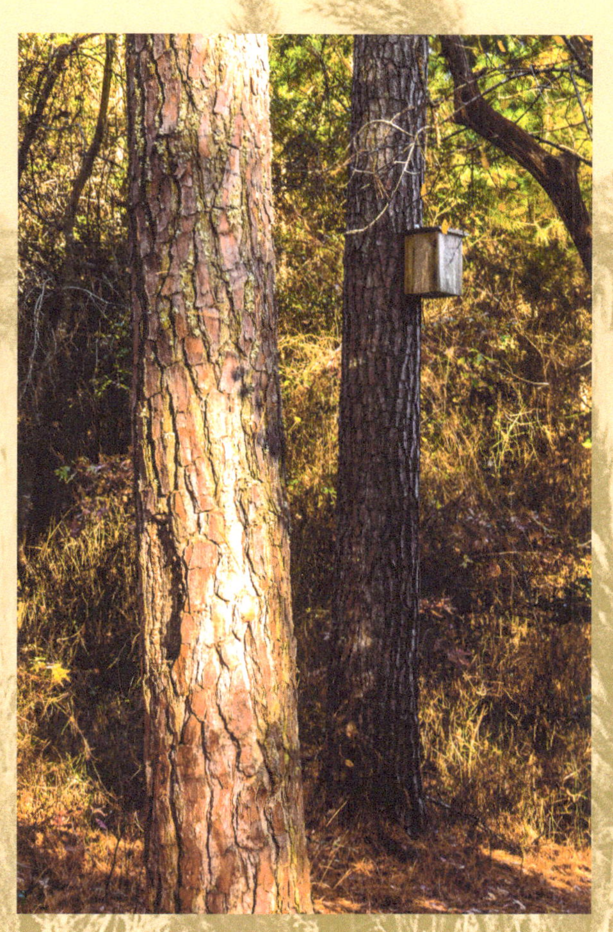 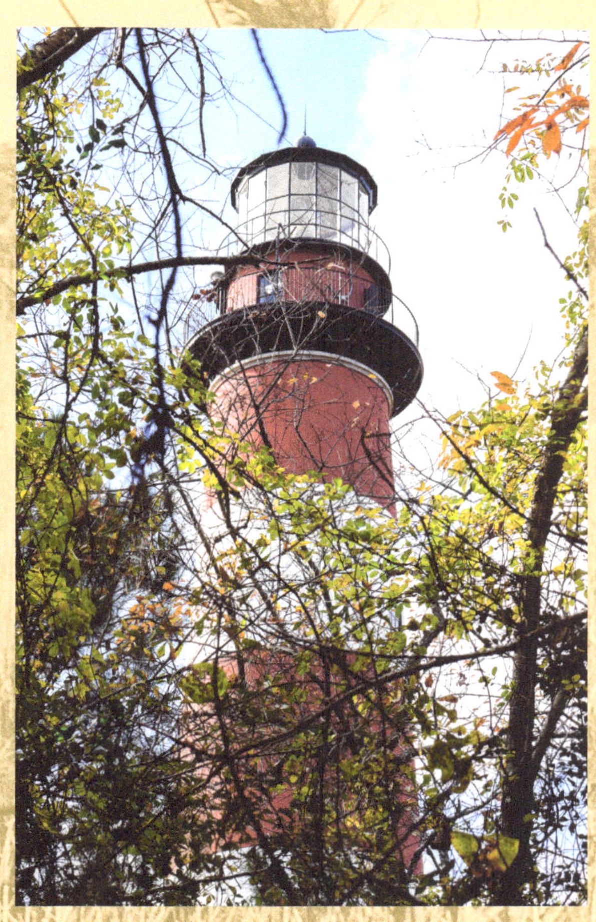

From the road, we walk through some woods, and the lighthouse comes into sight. In the past we were not permitted to climb up the steps in it, but it's been refurbished and it looks great. Come to Assateague Island and ascend its steps today to the very top!

Visit the Lighthouse

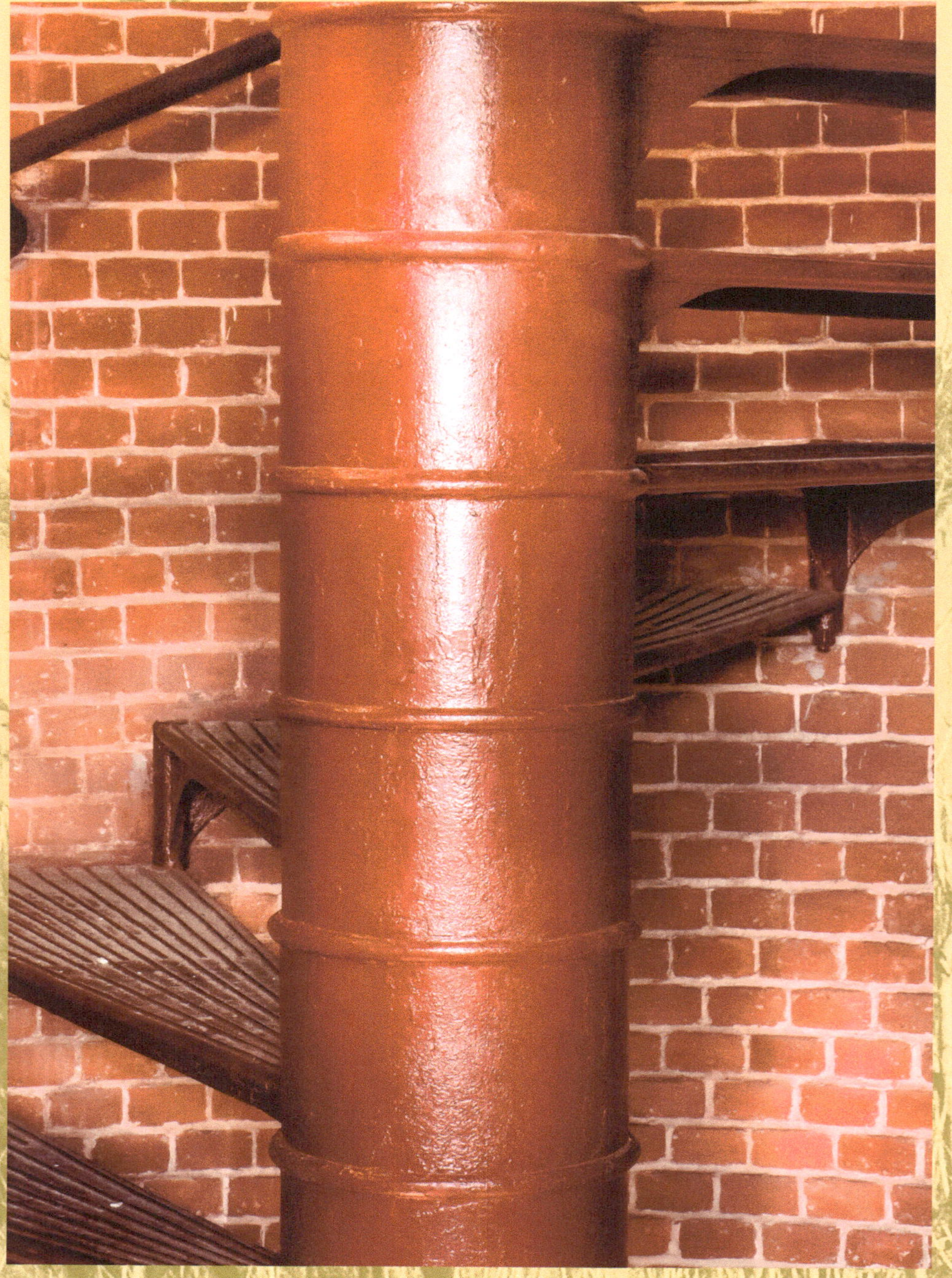

We're excited to climb to the top of the lighthouse, but we weary our way up the winding spiral staircase. Would you rather run up it in record time?

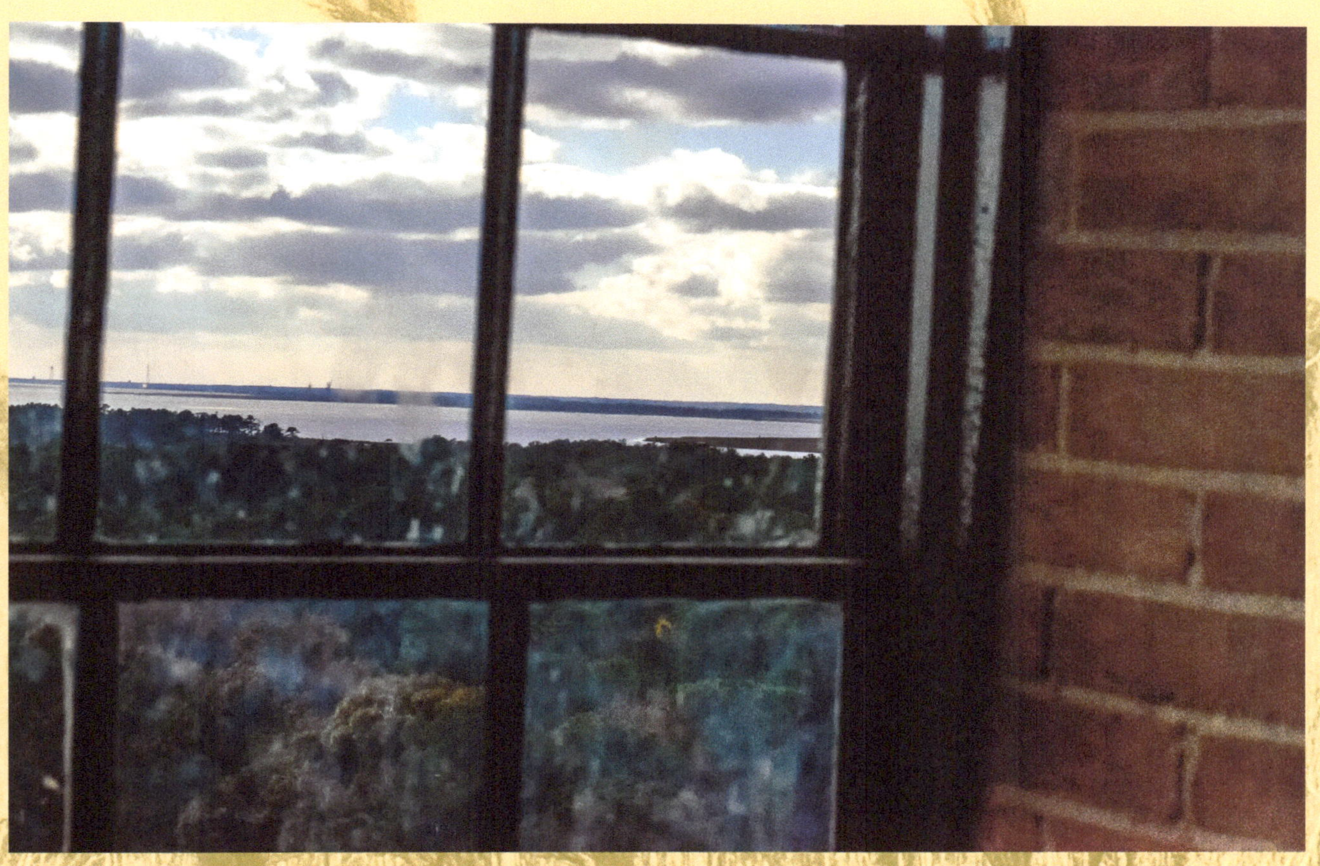

    On the way up, several hazy windows greet us with increasingly intriguing views.

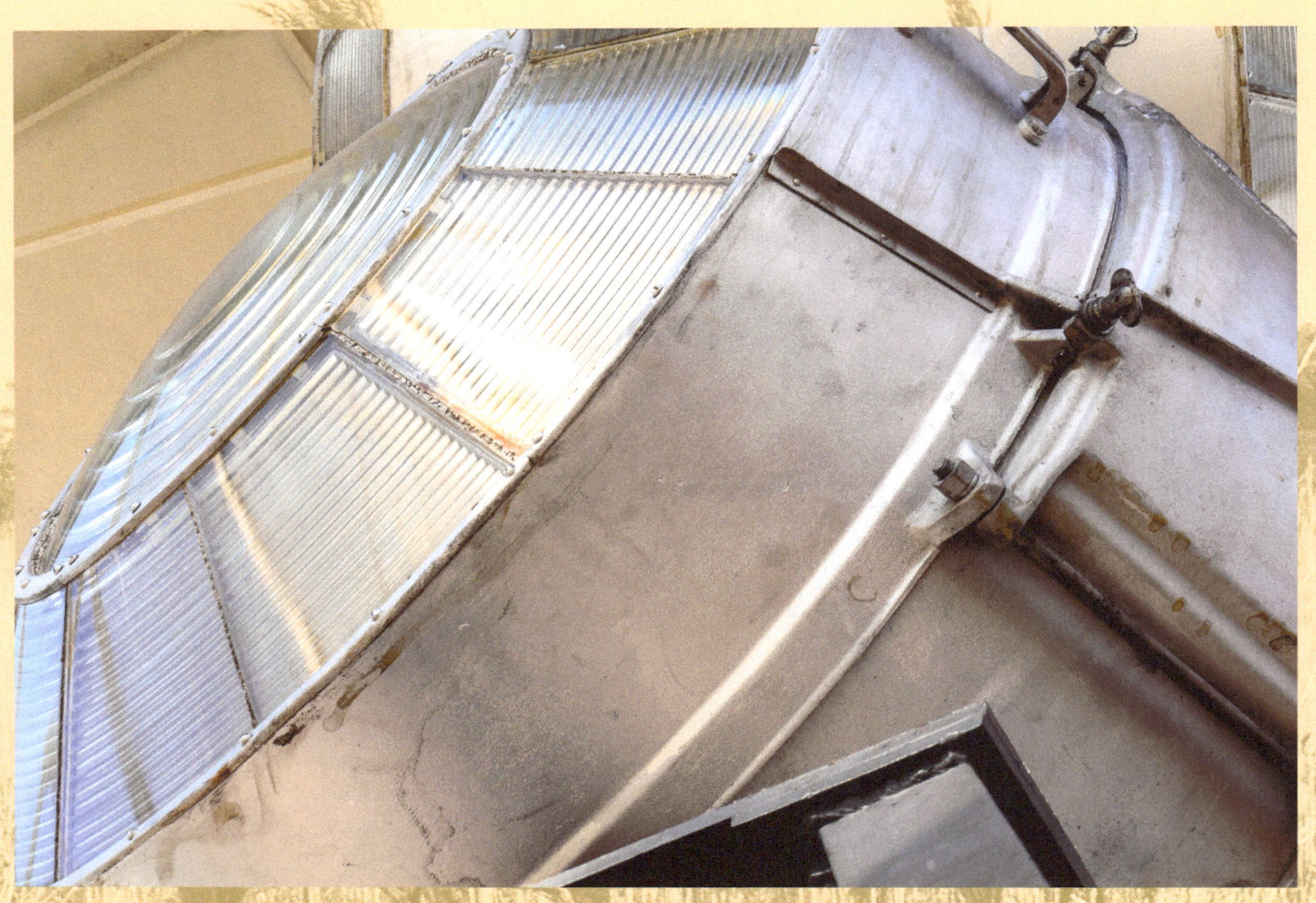

We finally arrive at the top, and are greeted by a large light with a Fresnel lens, which is designed to shine a narrow beam of light out to sea. This operating lighthouse is for more than just show.

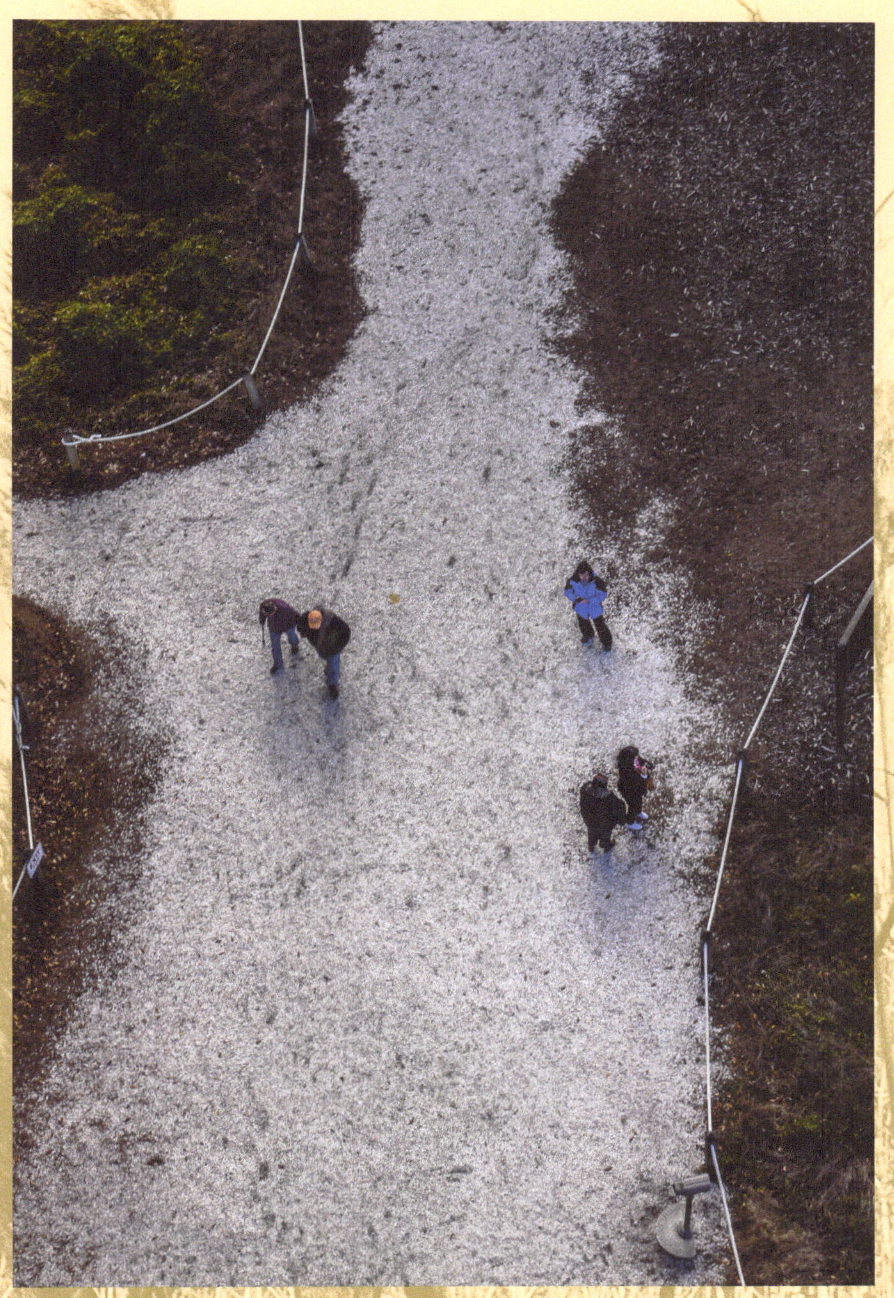

Stepping out on the deck, we are immediately over-come by vertigo from the height. When we look down, we see little ant-people coming to visit the lighthouse.

Visit the Lighthouse

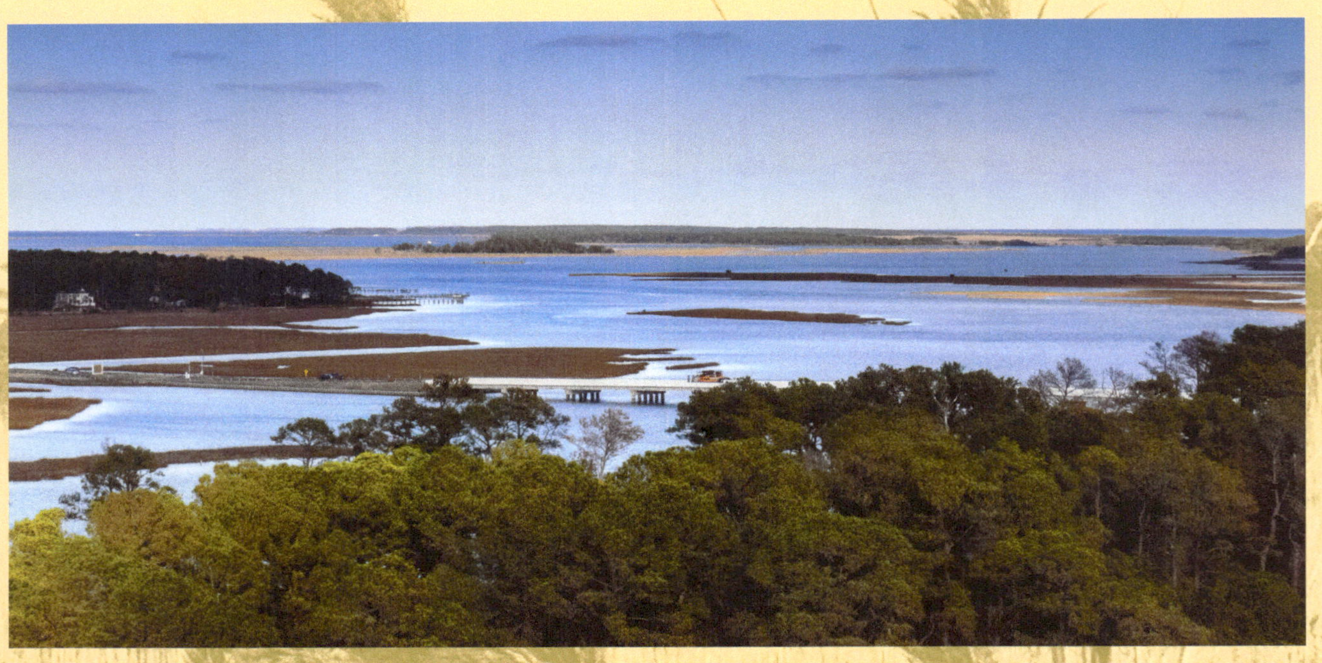

We then look out over the beautiful panorama of Assateague Channel and the bridge that crosses it. That's the same bridge that we had just recently traversed.

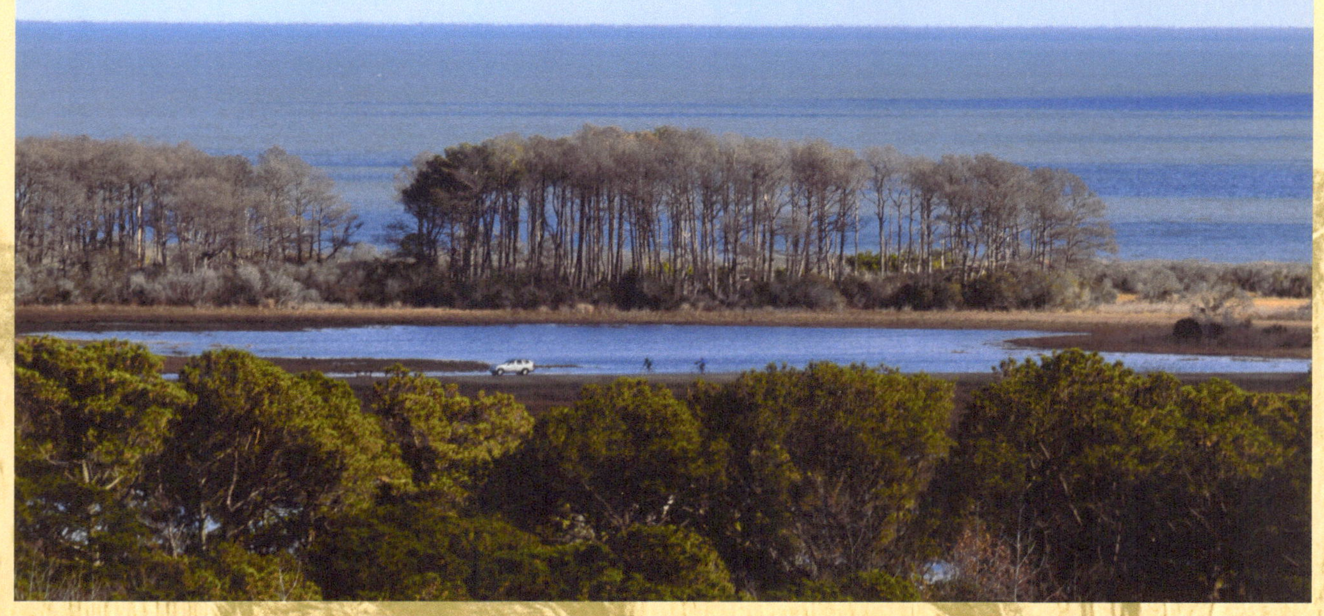

    Walking around to the other side of the lighthouse deck, we are overcome by the expanse of the Atlantic Ocean. Closer below us, we see a tidal pond, protected by a row of trees and vegetation. It looks as though people are enjoying touring around the pond, and perhaps getting close to wildlife.

Visit the Lighthouse

The views from the lighthouse include many birds, such as this turkey vulture. These birds may seem to pursue a disgusting lifestyle (as garbage collectors of the sky), but they are really quite majestic in flight.

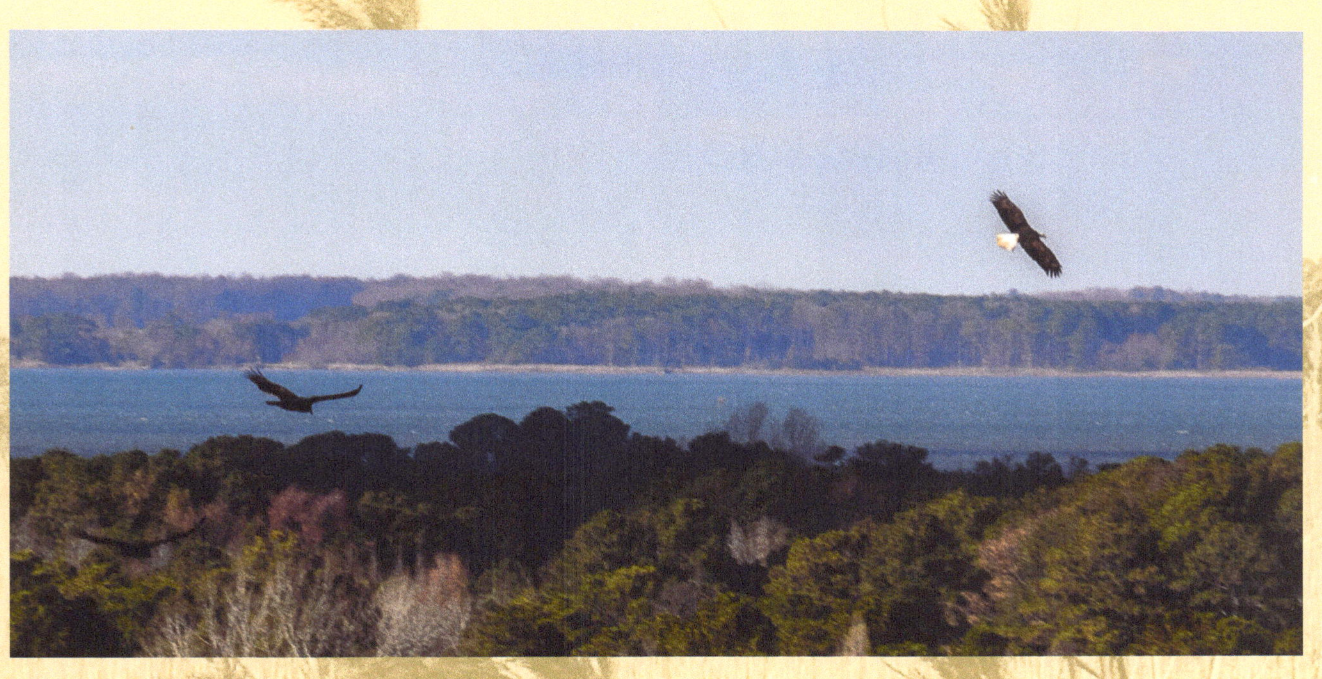

And they share the sky with our nation's iconic first bird, the bald eagle (right).

Chapter 5 -- Visit the Wildlife Loop

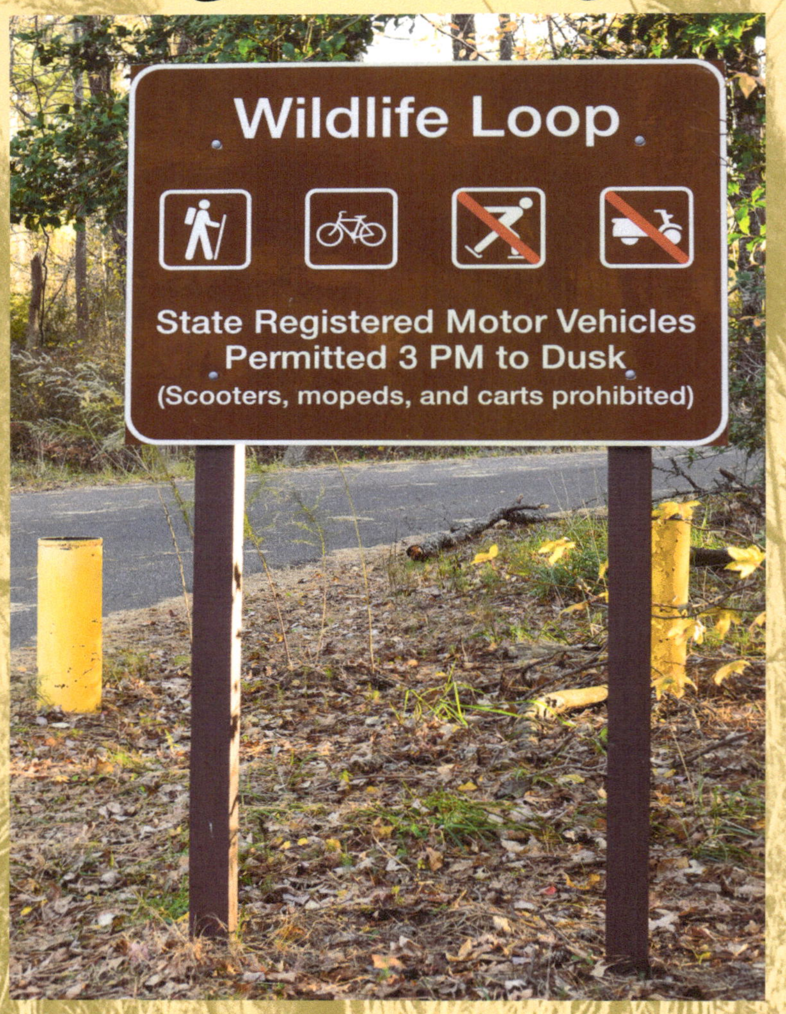

We love visiting the Wildlife Loop. It's reached a little sooner than the lighthouse after crossing the bridge. The Loop road encircles Snow Goose Pond, and it has longer hours during Thanksgiving week.

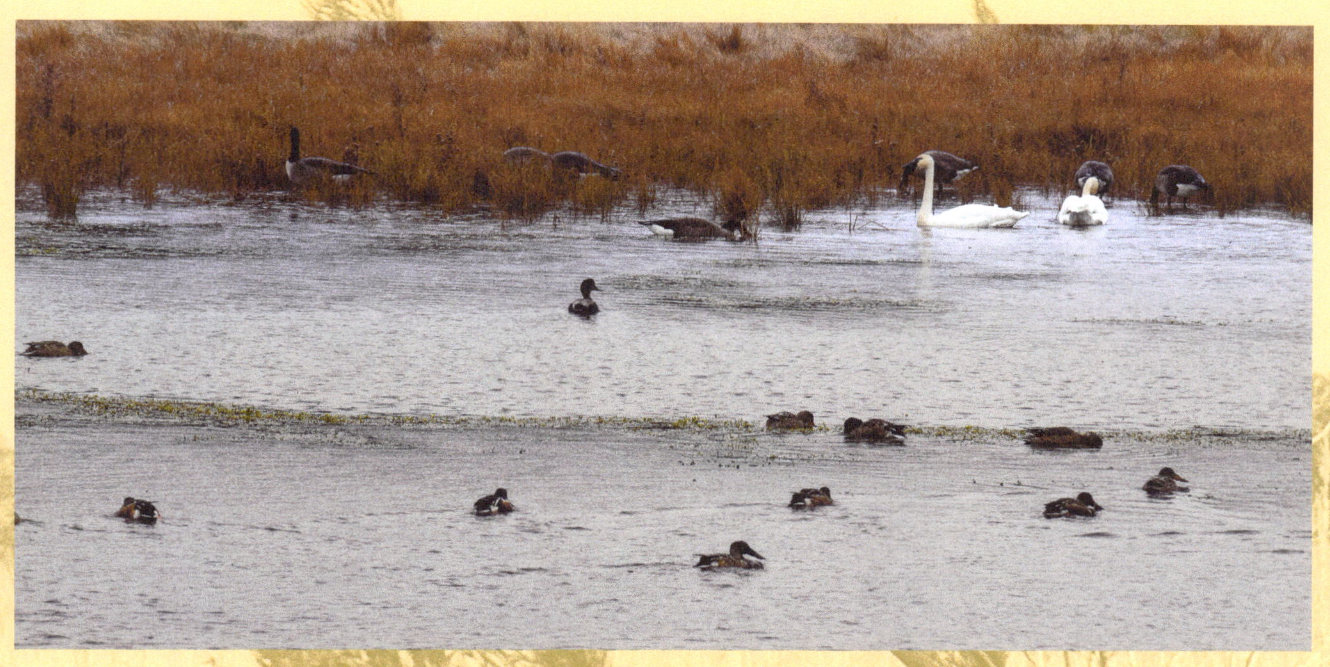

We expect snow geese, of course, which we've enjoyed in past years, but we're disappointed. Where can they be?

We do, however, find many other water fowl. Canada geese are lurking at the edge of the marsh, along with a pair of tundra swans. Most of the ducks swimming around are northern shoveler ducks, with quite distinctive bills. The one duck swimming away in the center is a Gadwall duck, who sometimes steals food from other ducks — what a thief!

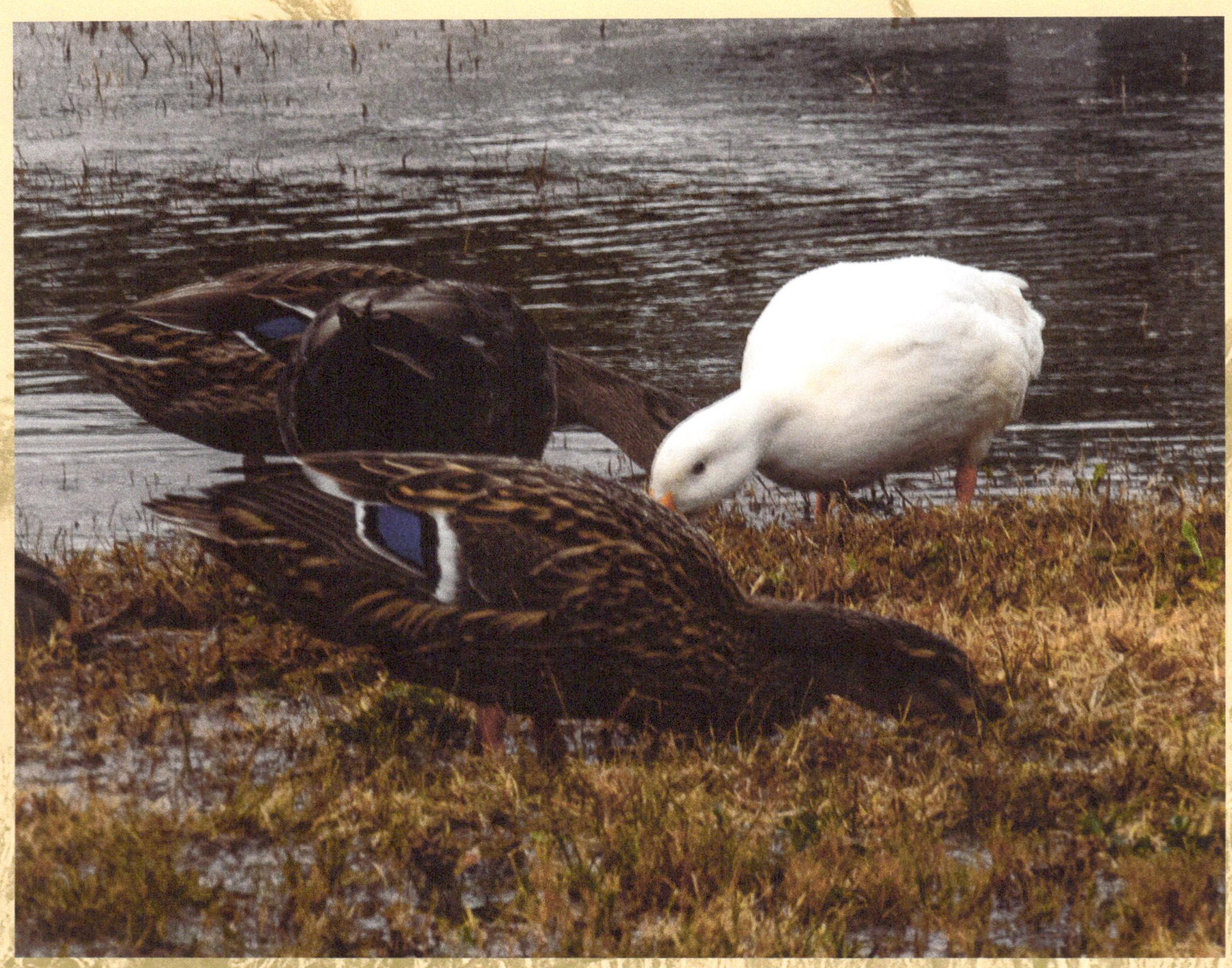

There are a wide variety of hungry ducks. Here are three mallard females and one American Pekin duck (the white one) that somehow escaped from the duck farm. Talk about free-range!

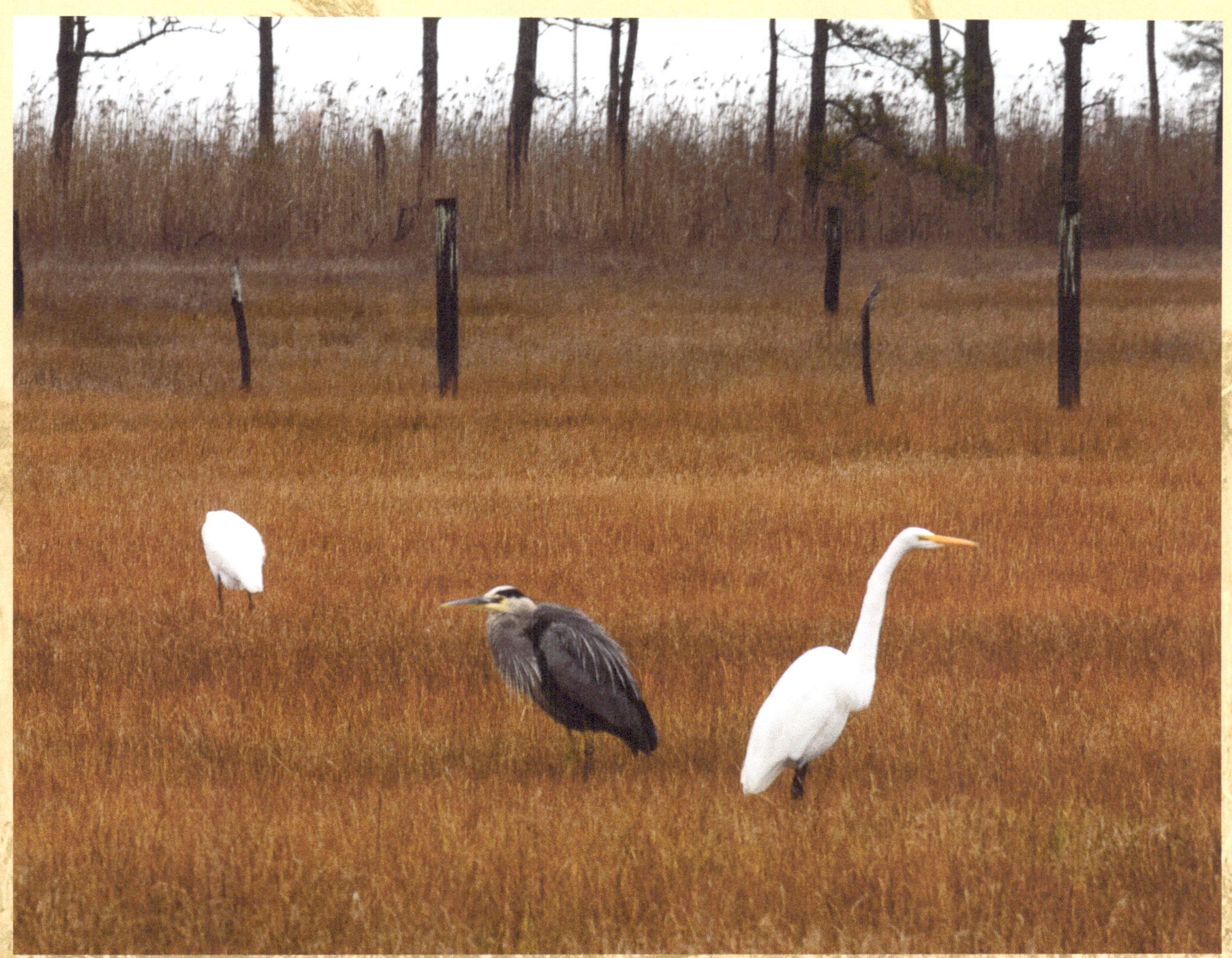

And the egrets and herons are hanging around, pretending not to notice each other.

Visit the Wildlife Loop

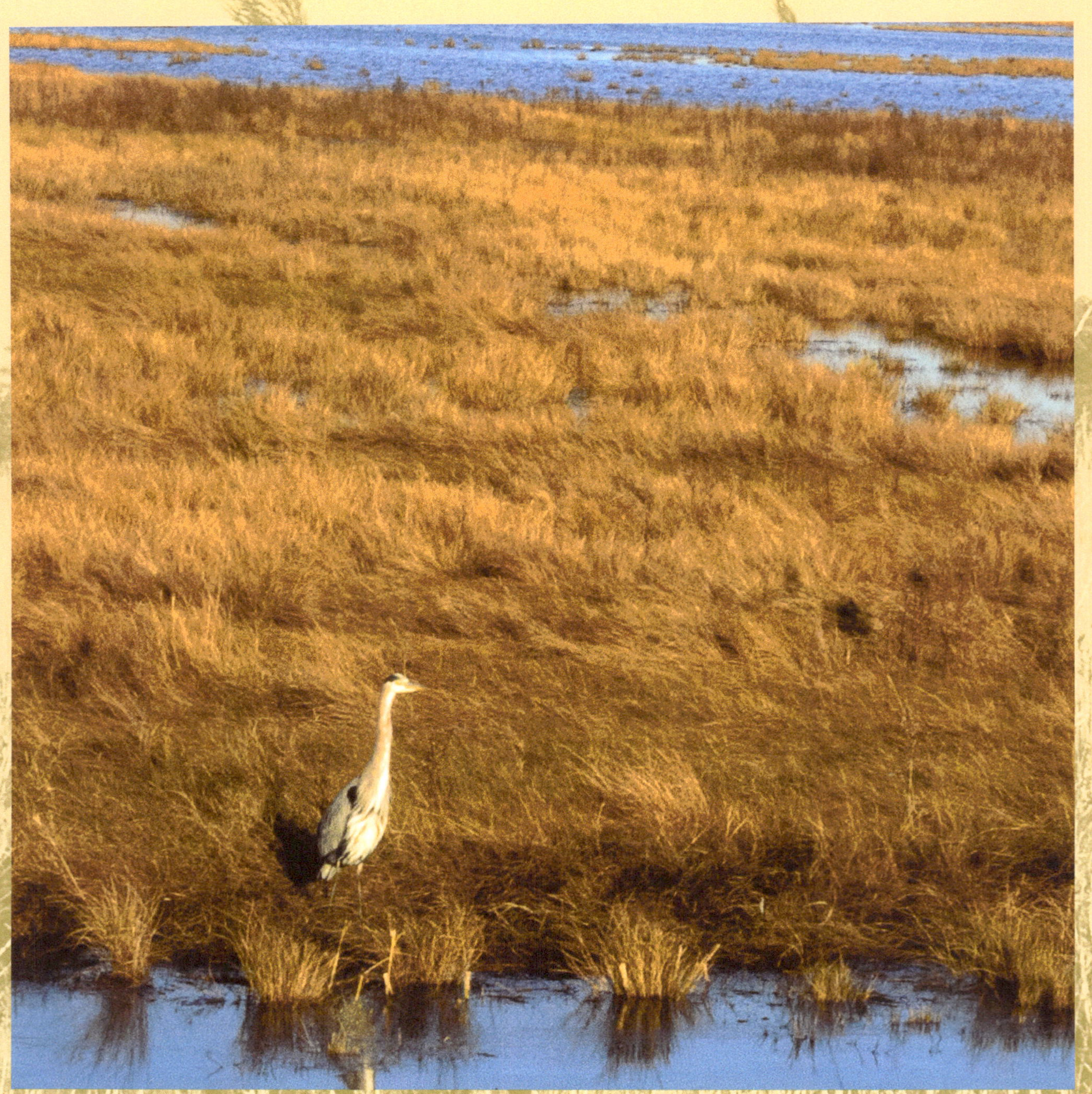

This great white egret patrols the marshes ...

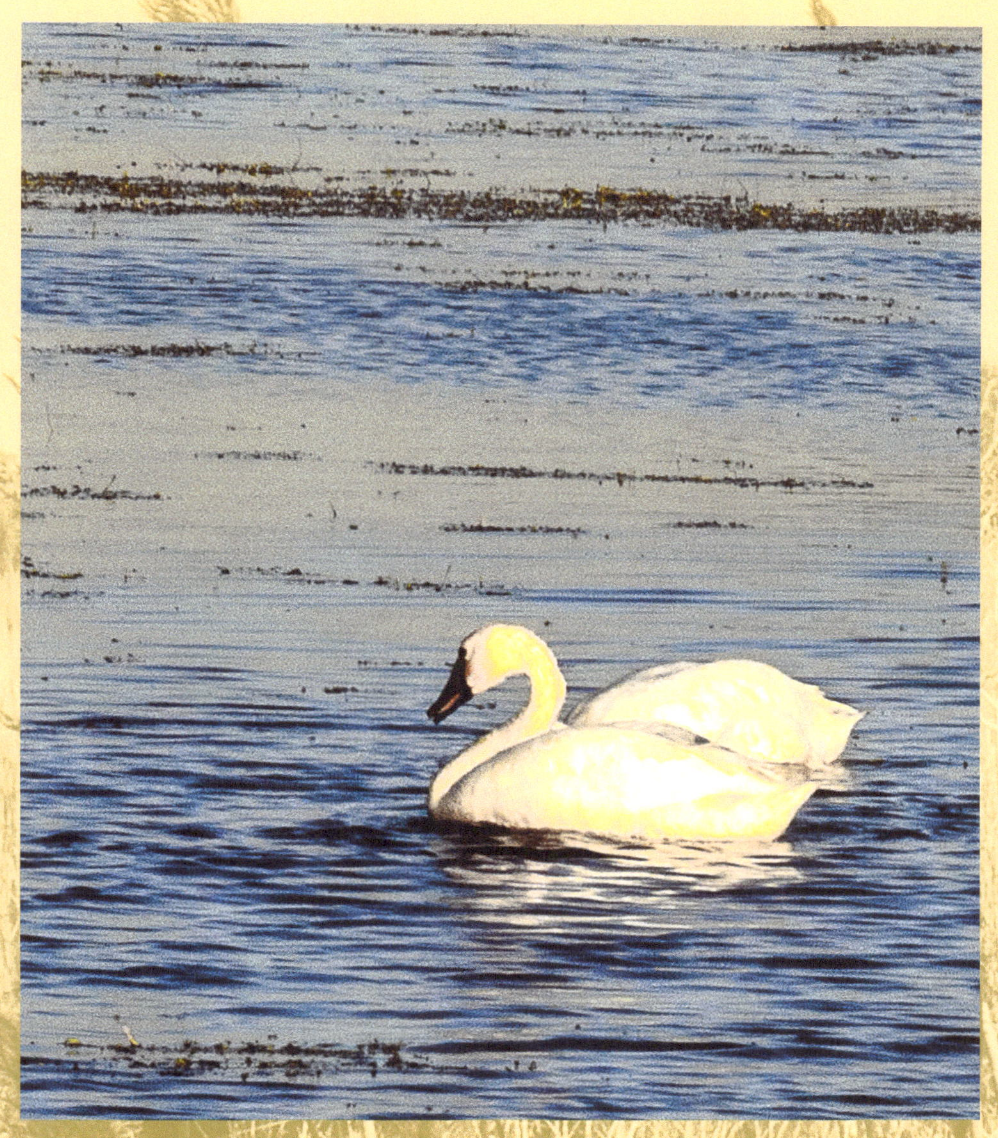

... while two tundra swans (one is dabbling for pond vegetation to eat) enjoy the solitude of Snow Goose Pond, now evacuated of snow geese. These birds are also trying to ignore all those tourist birders. They don't feel any need for all that attention anyway.

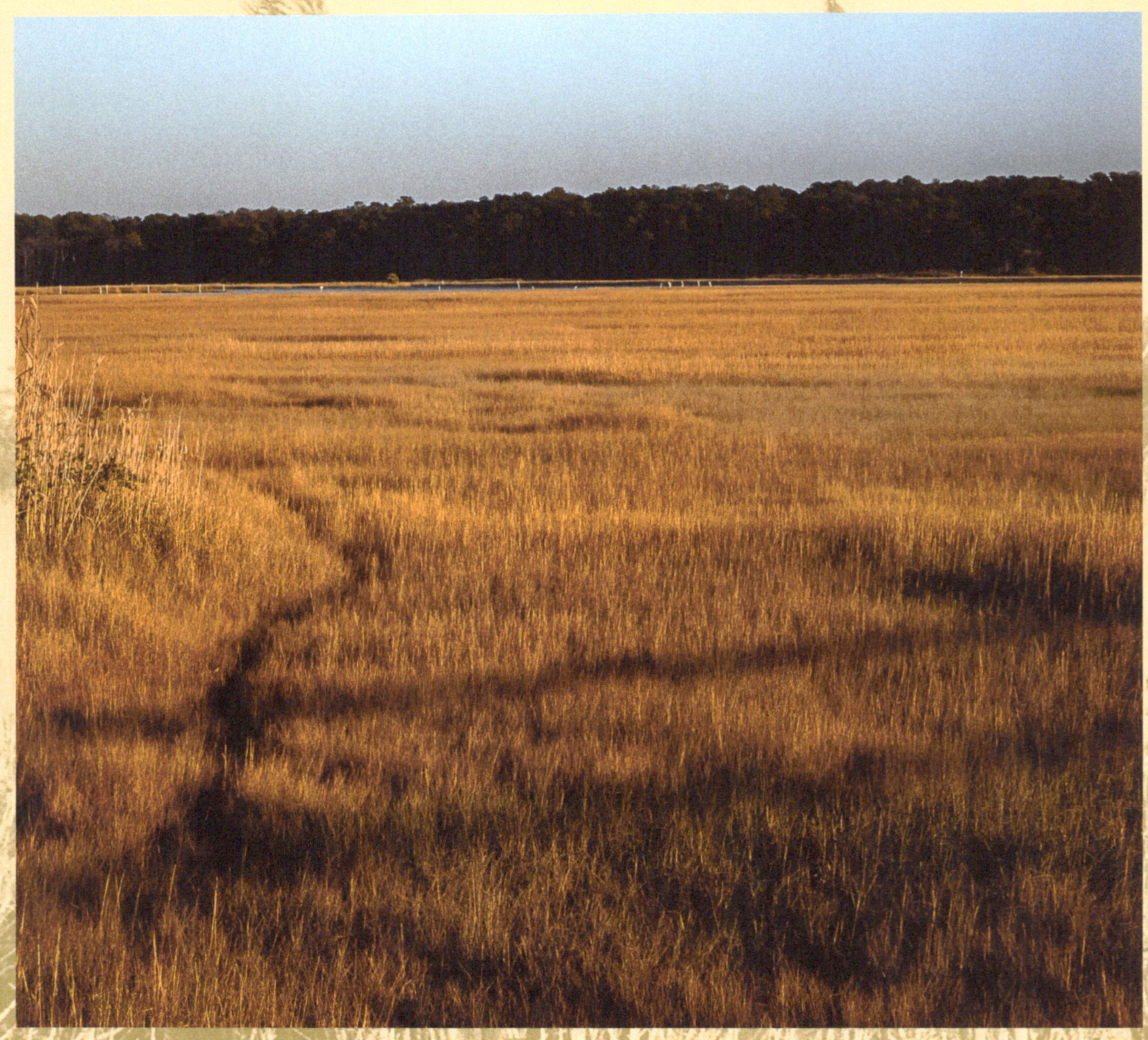

The views from much of the Wildlife Loop road are of marshland: not quite land and not quite water, but full of life. Can you see the great white egrets in the distance, on the horizon of this salt marsh?

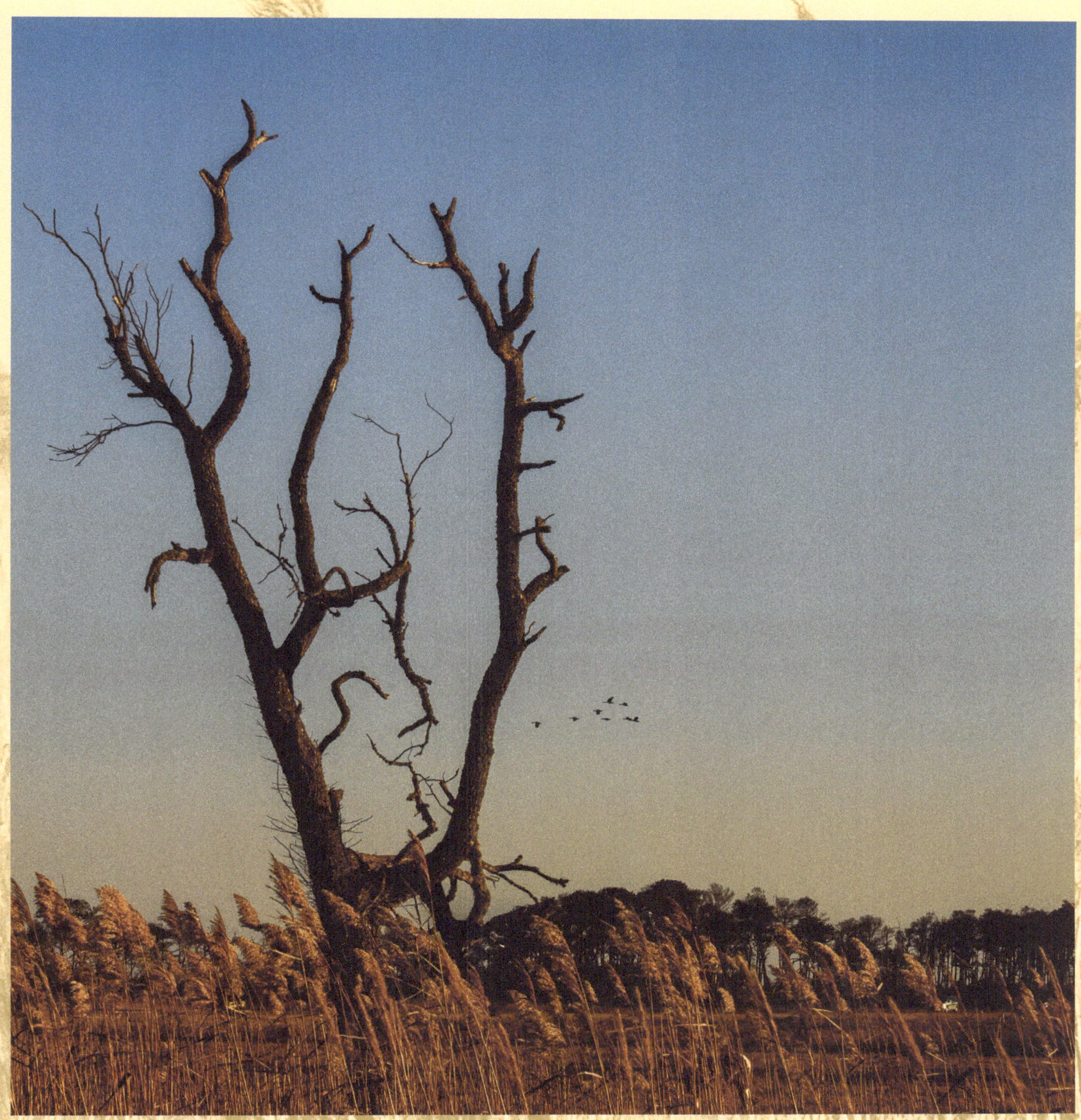

And even death makes room for life.

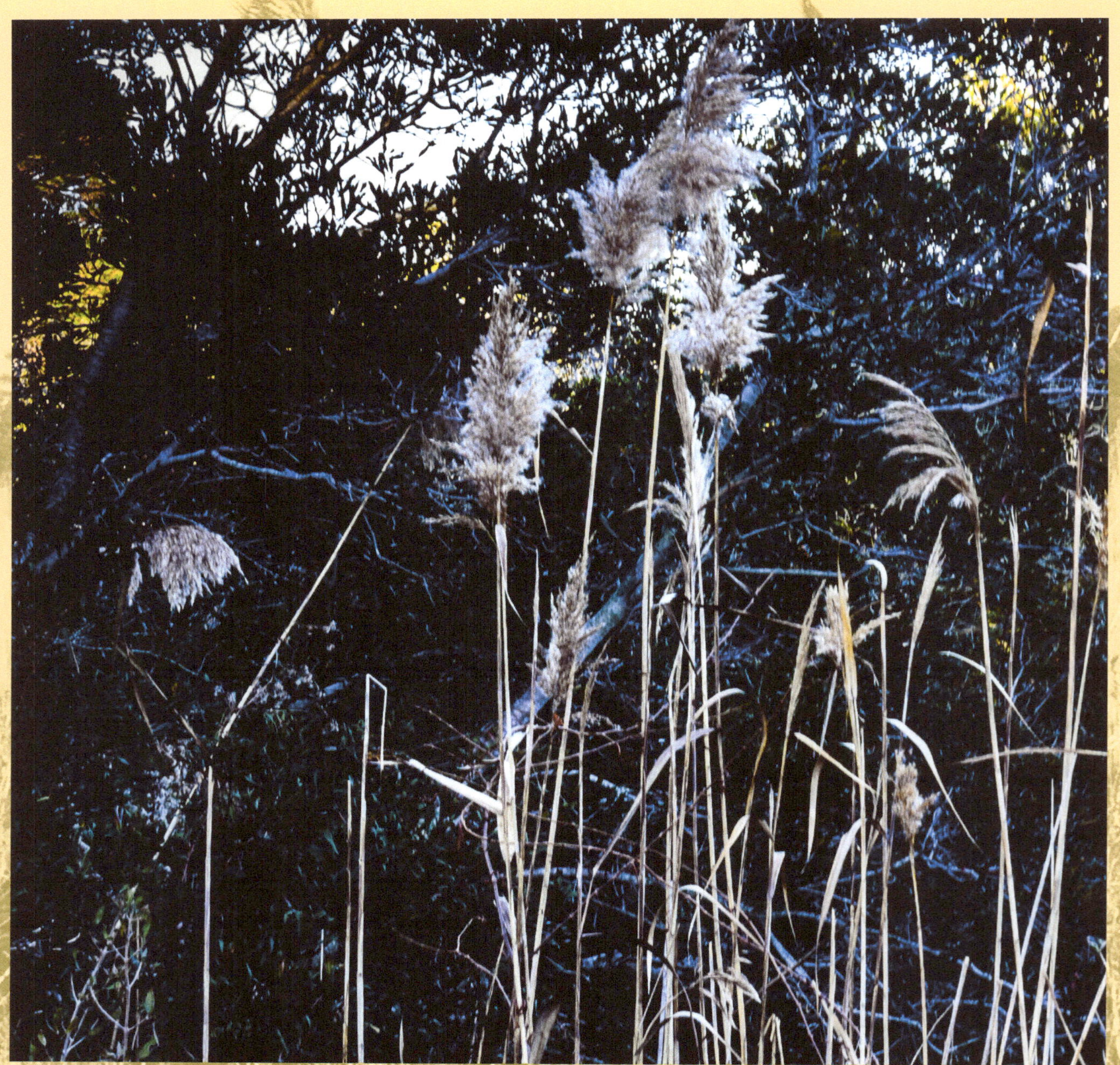

There are also many marshland plants, such as these plume grasses ...

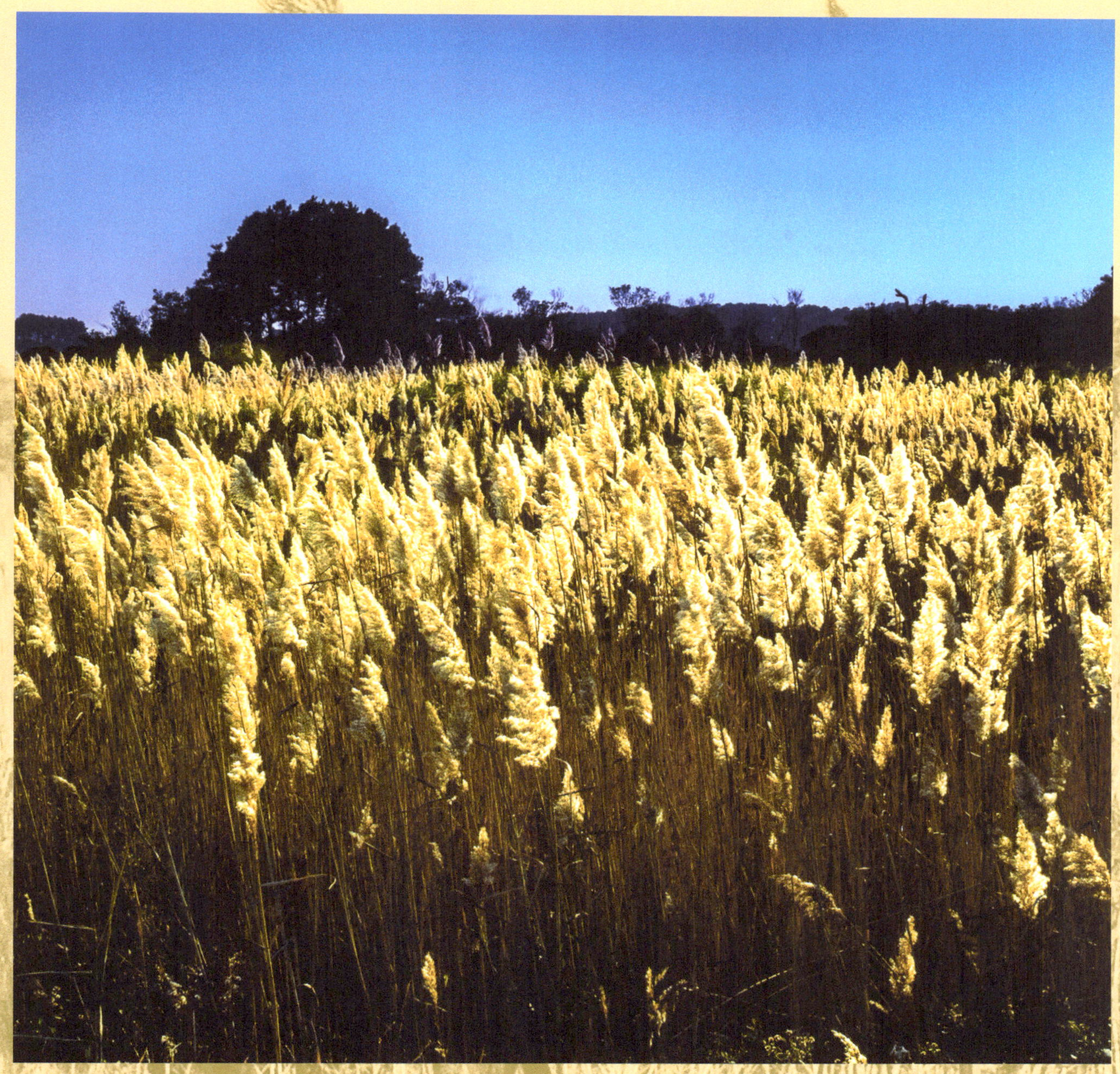

... and these common reeds.

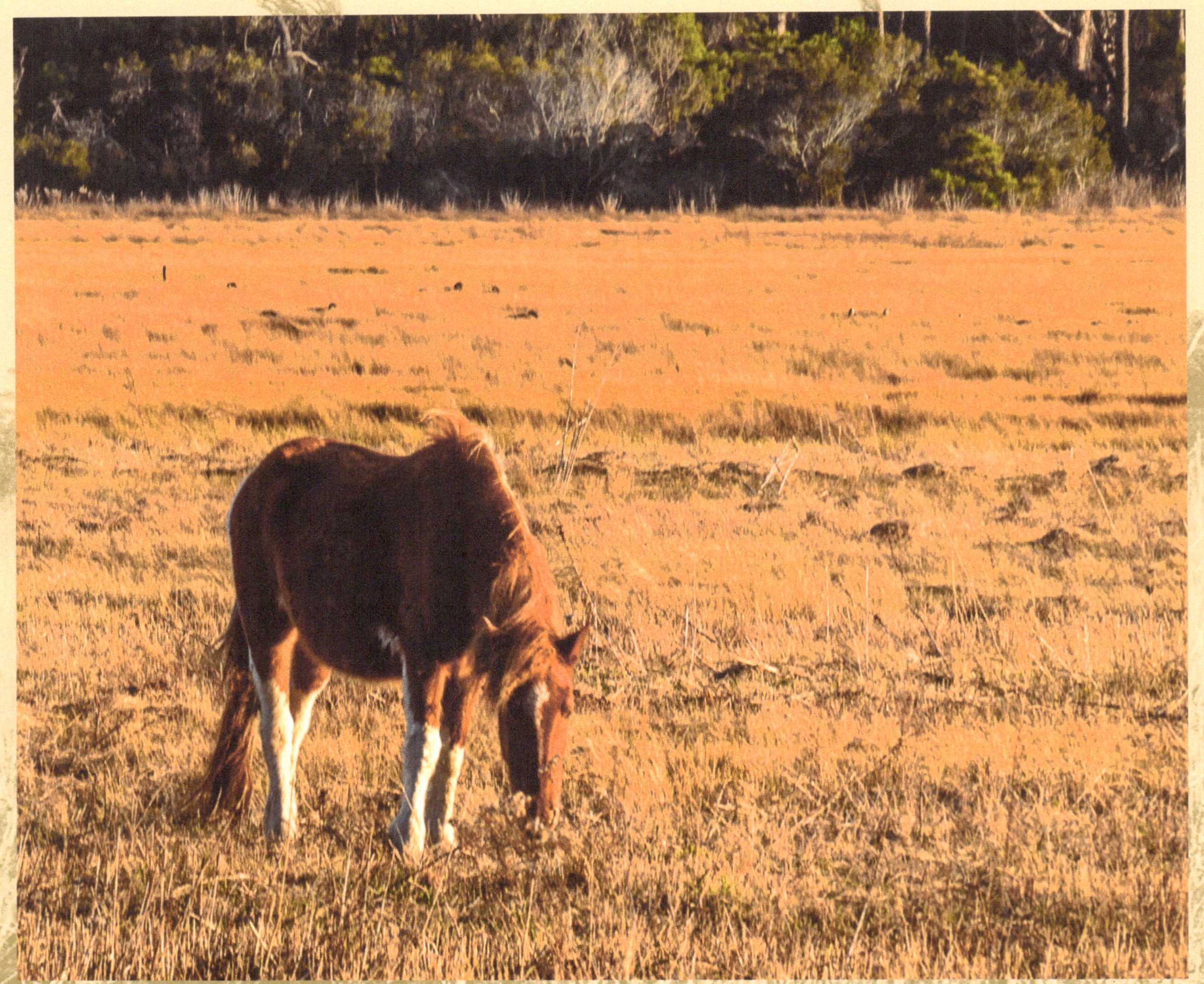

We're thrilled to see this pony. It's standing in a field near the pond munching on the wild grasses. But aren't there supposed to be lots of ponies? Don't worry, there are many of them, and they'll show up in the next chapter.

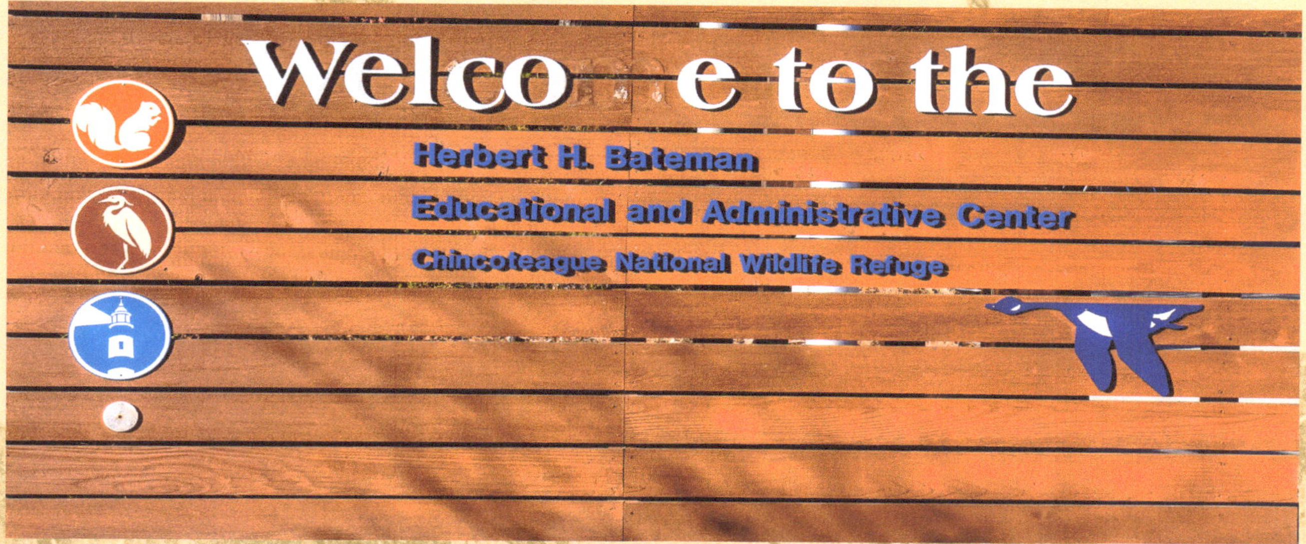

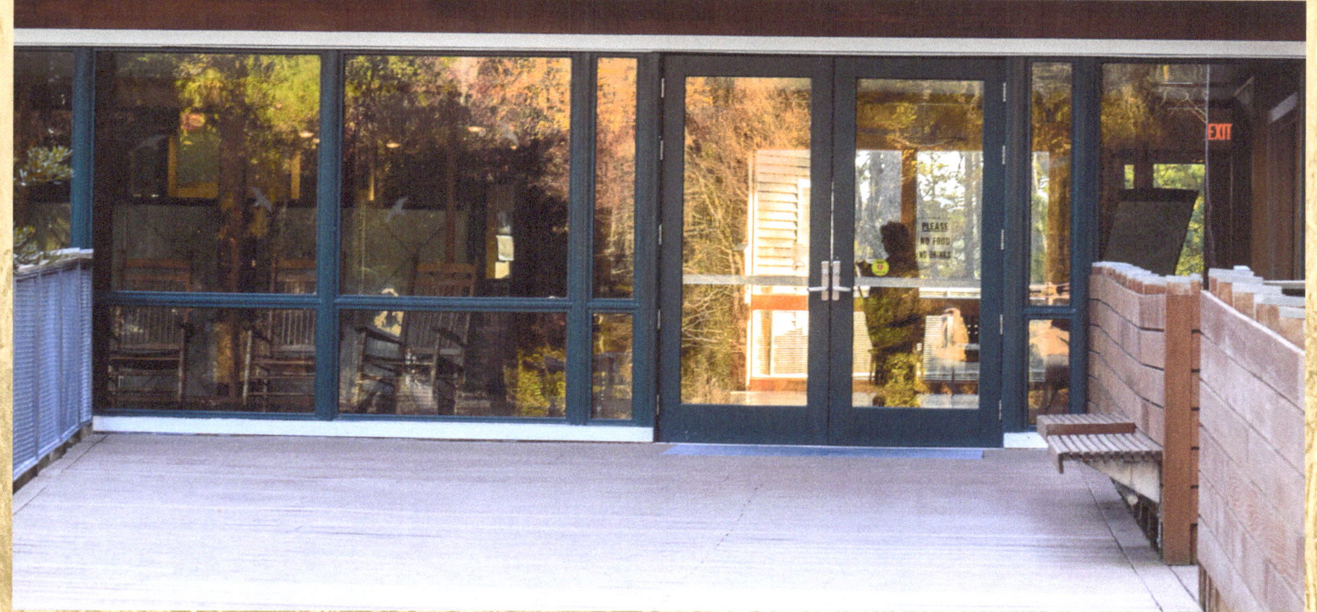

Around the corner from the Wildlife Loop is the Bateman Center, which features nature-oriented displays, knowledgeable speakers, and various activities to better understand this wonderful wildlife refuge.

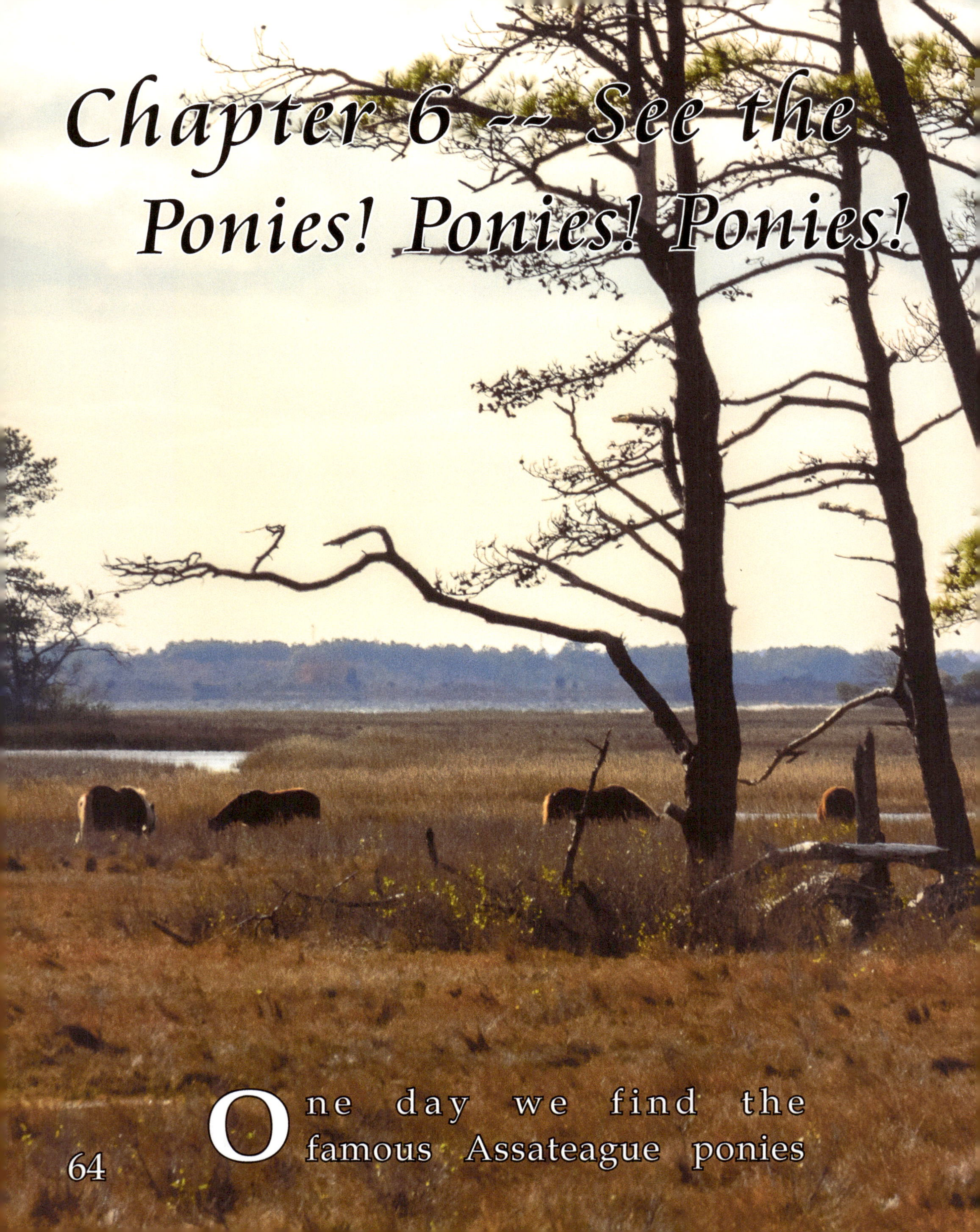
Chapter 6 -- See the
Ponies! Ponies! Ponies!

One day we find the
famous Assateague ponies

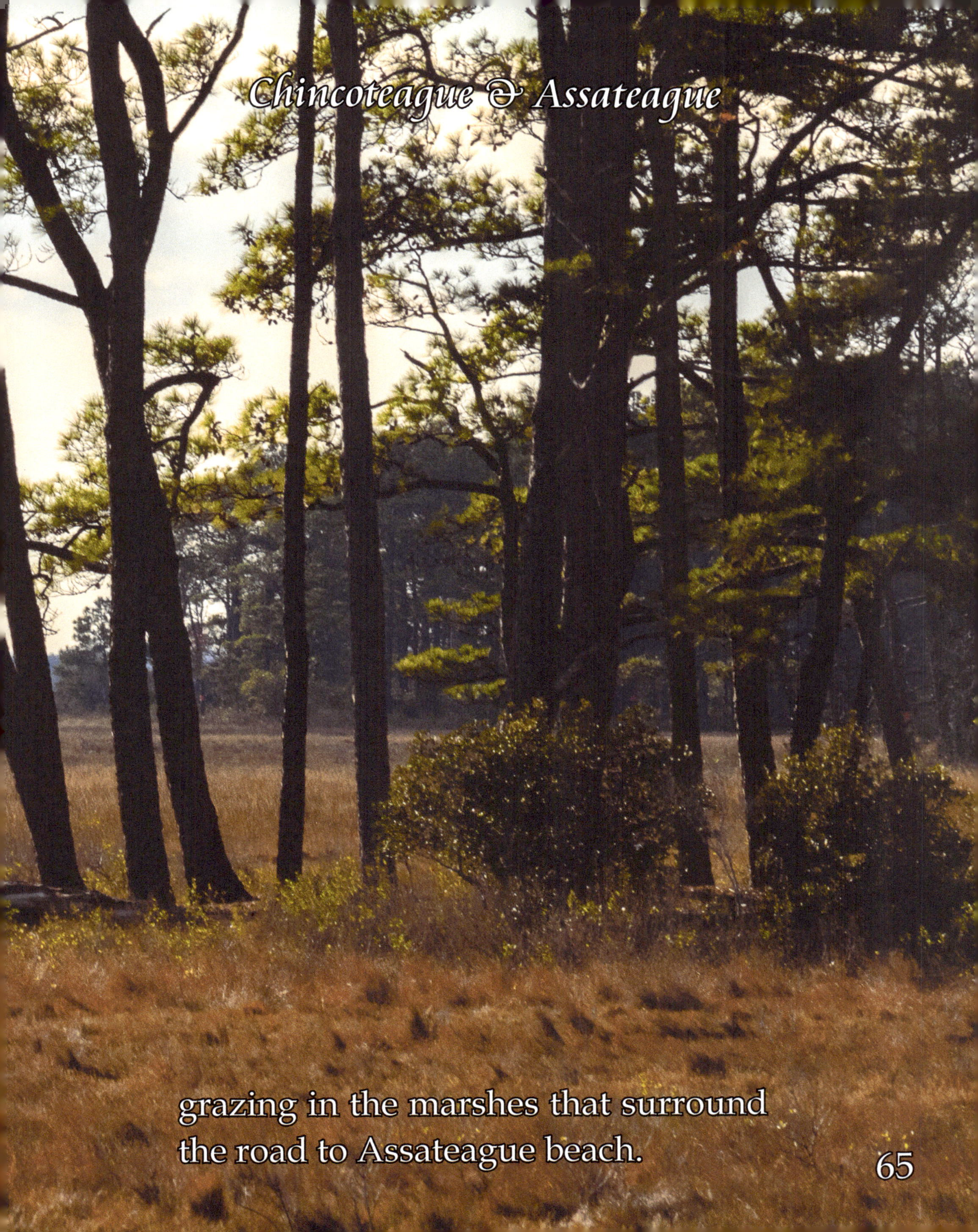

grazing in the marshes that surround
the road to Assateague beach.

See the Ponies! Ponies! Ponies!

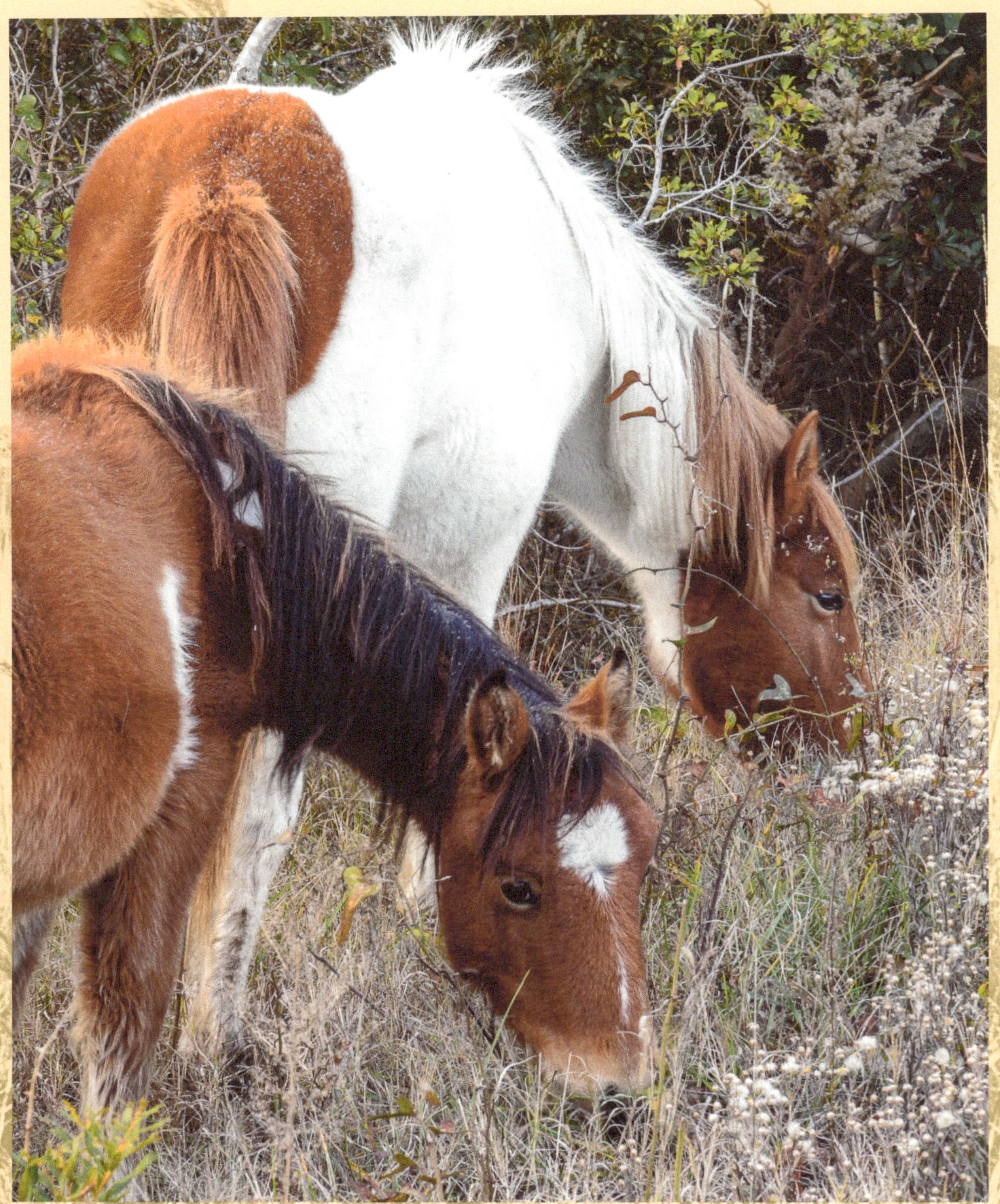

These ponies are eating their lunch.

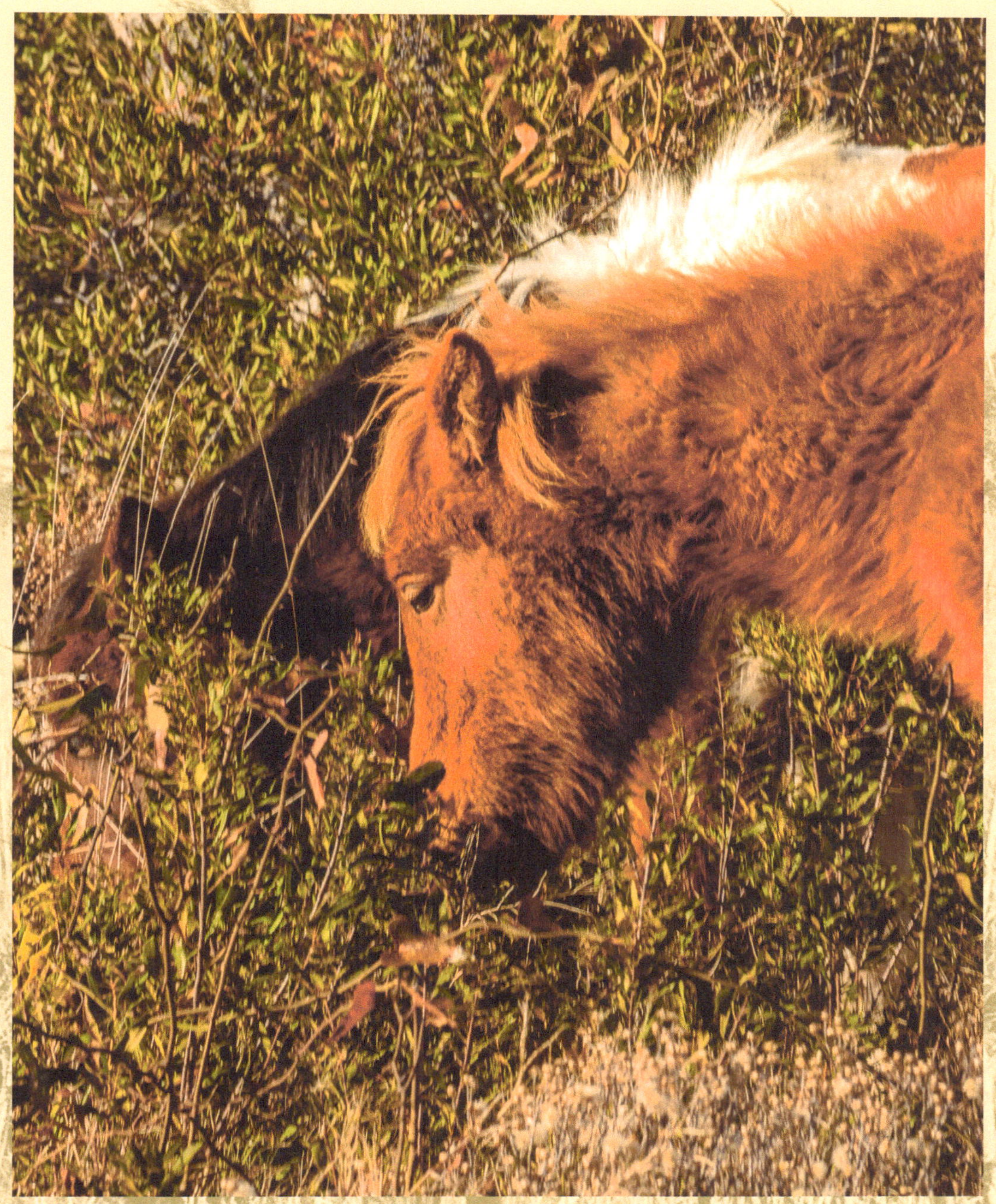

There is really a lot of diversity in appearance of the Assateague ponies, but they all agree that marsh plants are yummy.

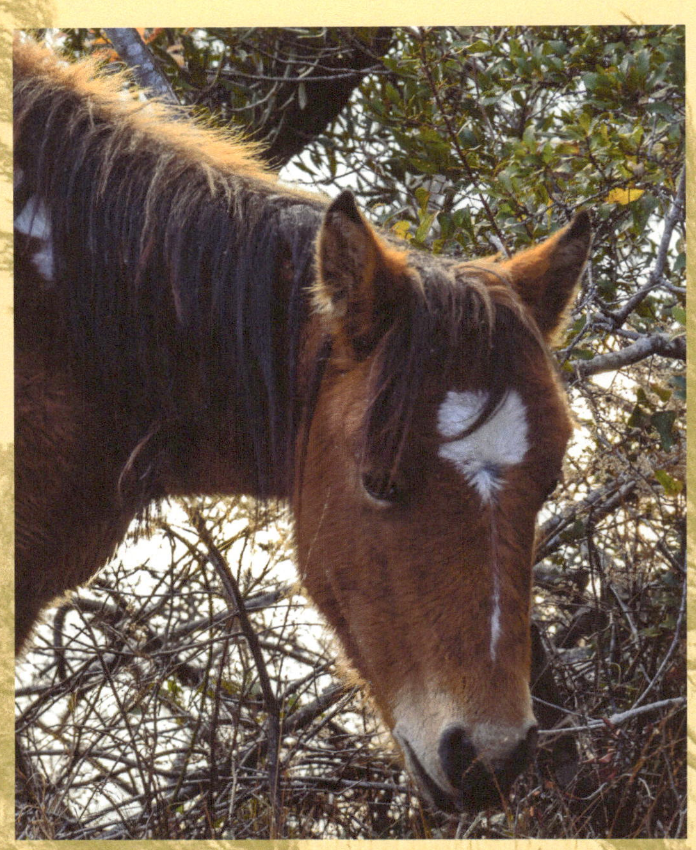

There was a time long ago when locals owned ponies, but if taxes were too burdensome, then the owners released the ponies on the island, knowing the ponies could eat the vegetation in the marshes, and the owners could gather up their ponies later whenever they wanted. Perhaps, however, the owners sometimes forgot about them, and herds of the ponies grew.

Well—this is another origin story for the ponies, but not as romantic as Spanish Galleon wrecks offshore. The fire department owns the ponies now.

Chincoteague & Assateague

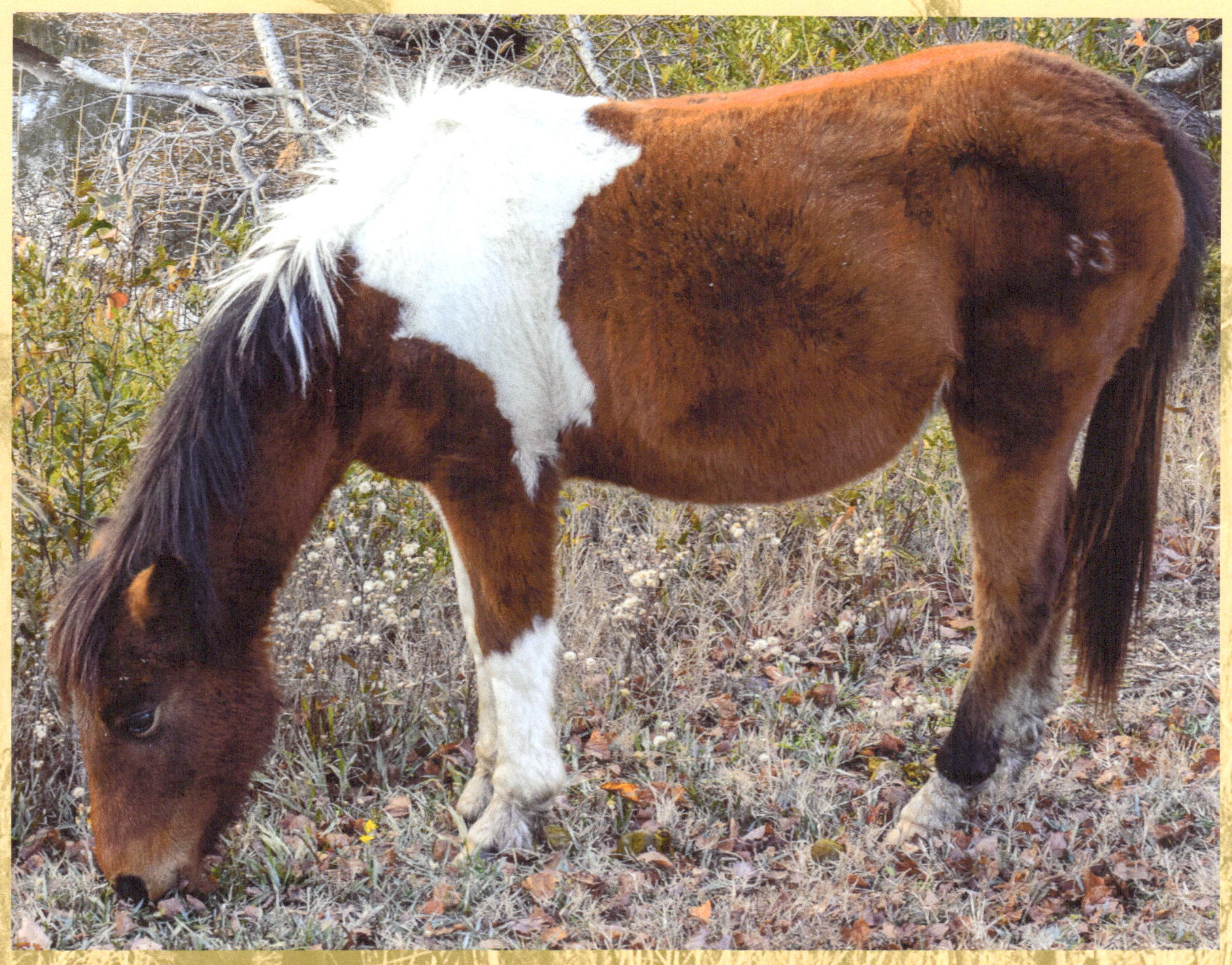

This mare is not pregnant; all the ponies are fat like this due to their diet of vegetation that is high in salt from the nearby ocean.

See the Ponies! Ponies! Ponies!

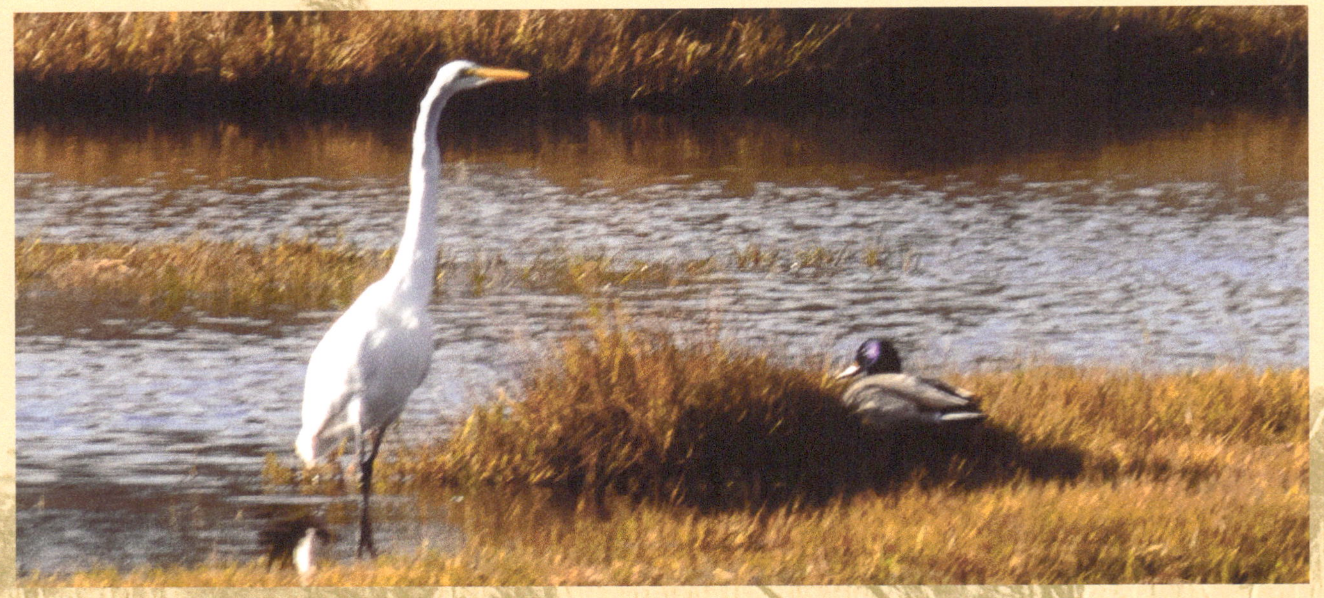

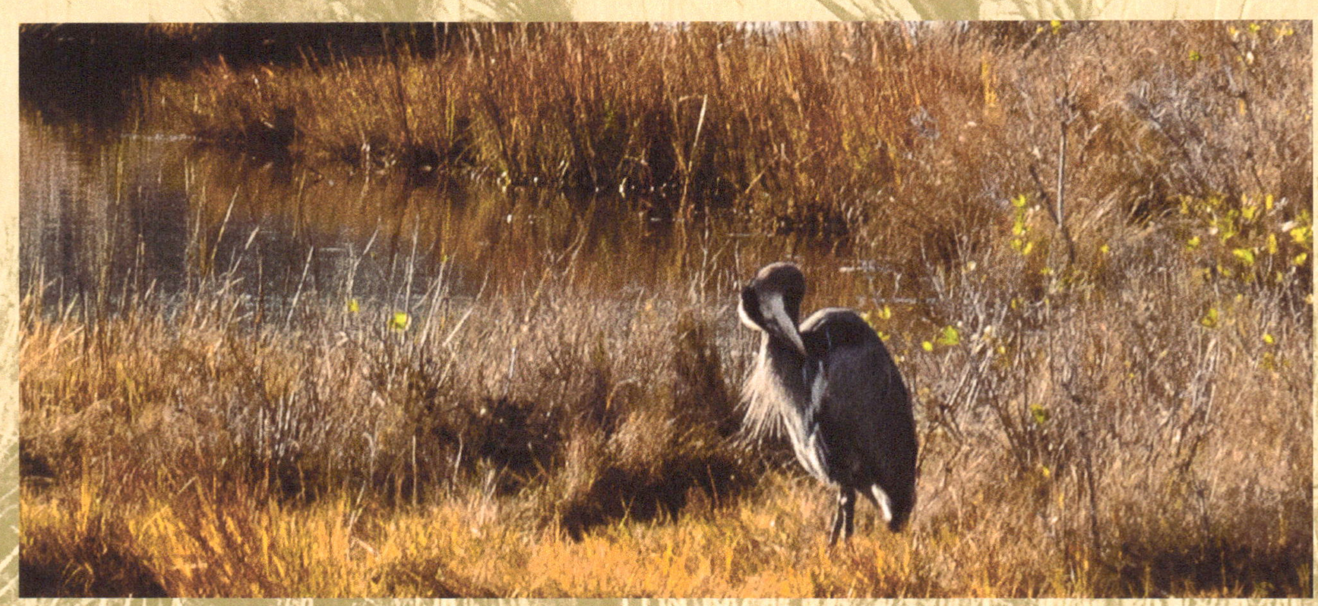

Wait a moment, these aren't ponies! Well, naturally, birds are sharing the marshes with the ponies, like this great white egret and mallard duck (top), and great blue heron (above).

70

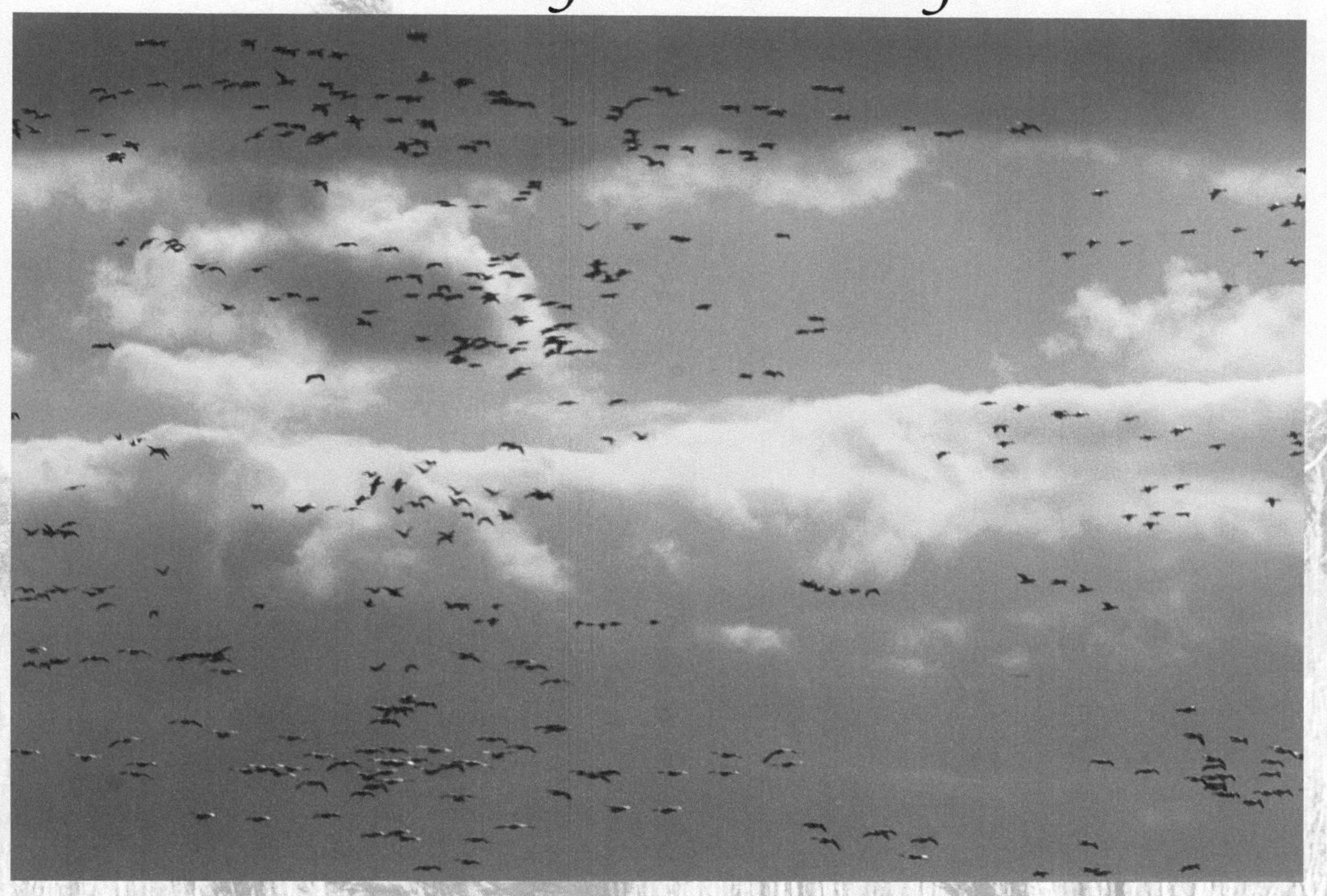

And the birds are also in the skies above.
The birds are just everywhere.

Chapter 7 -- Explore The Beach

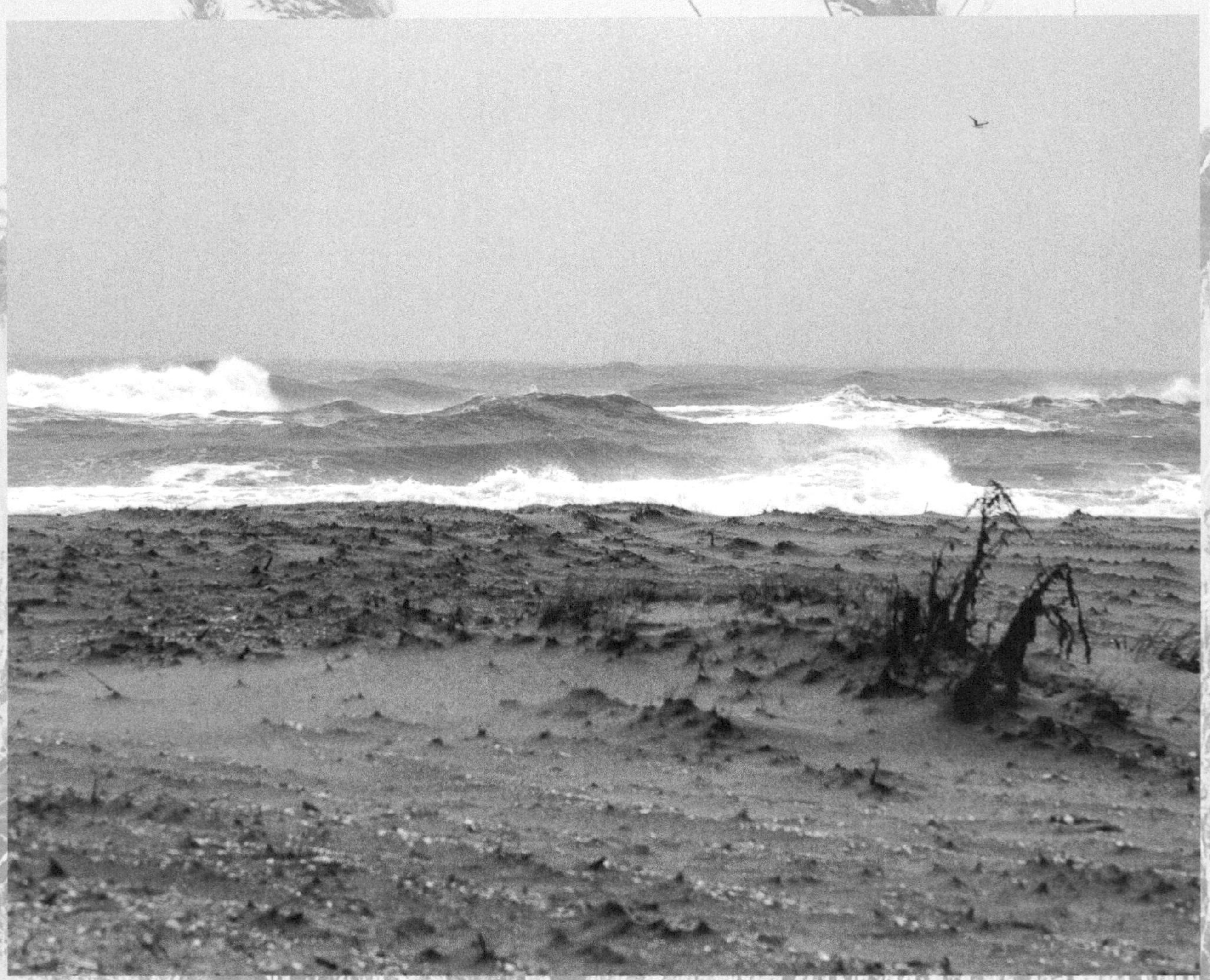

On this day we walk along the Assateague Island beach a bit.

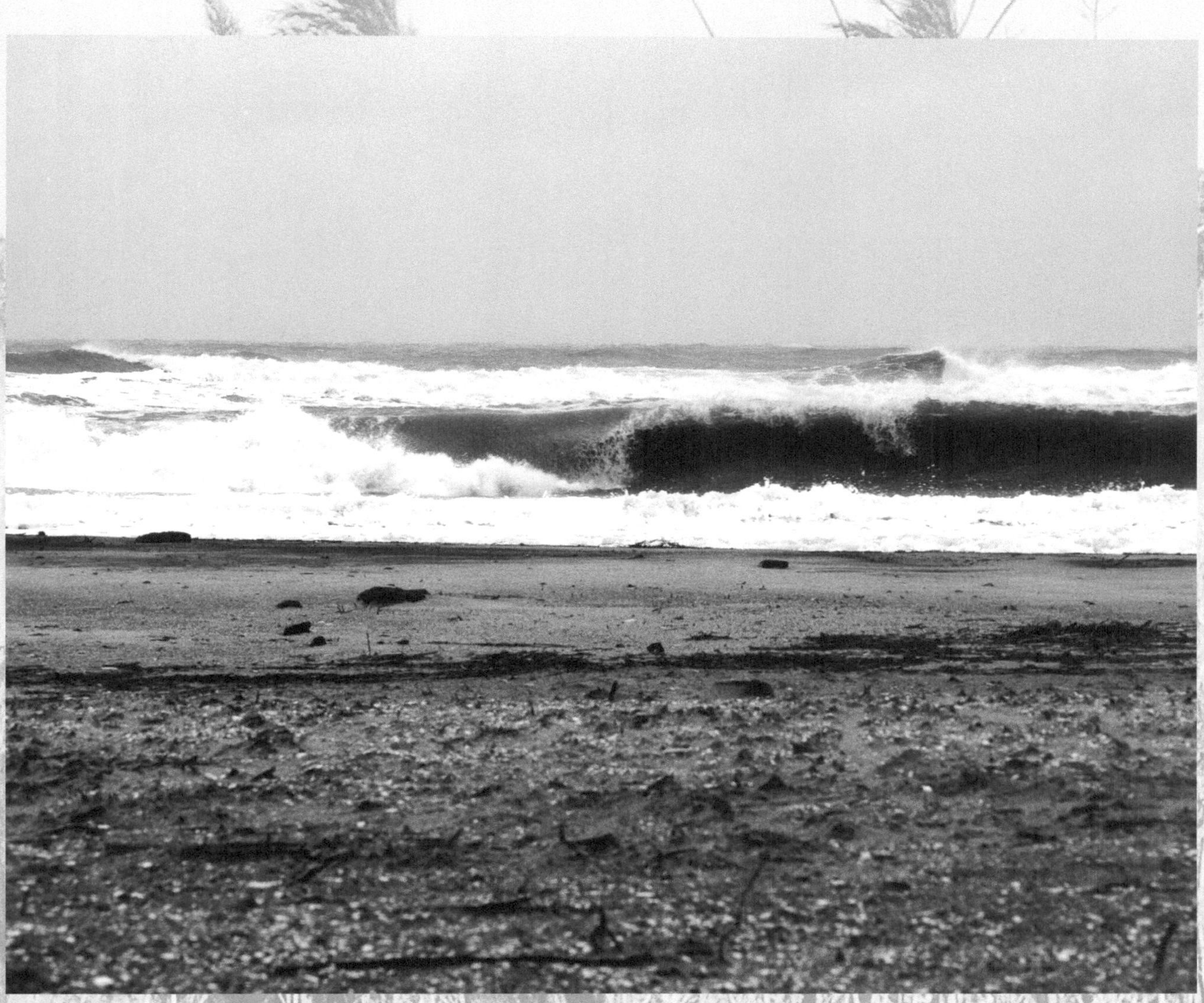

It's overcast, and a spectacularly bad day for swimming. The ocean looks pretty rough!

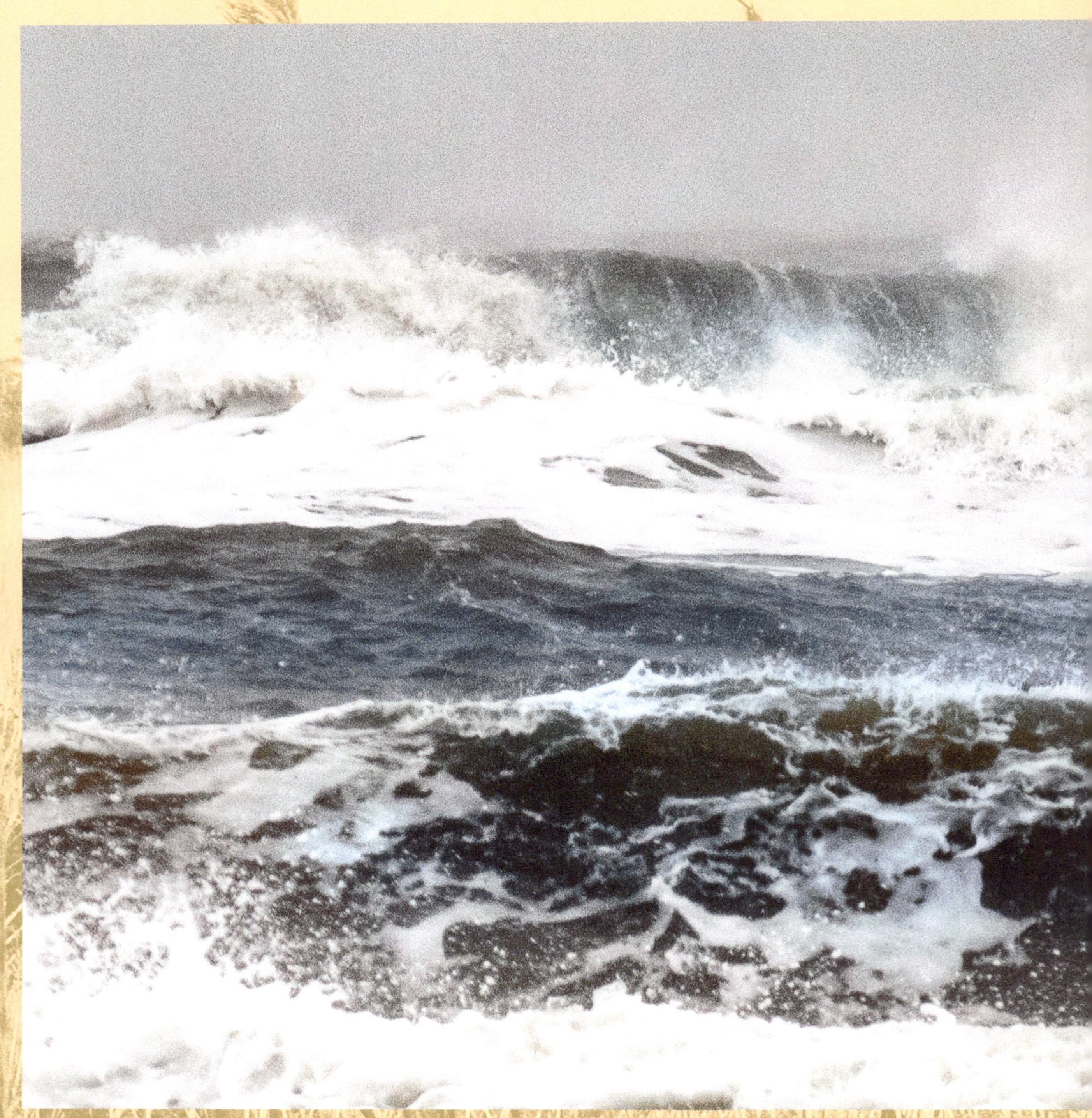

It does indeed ...

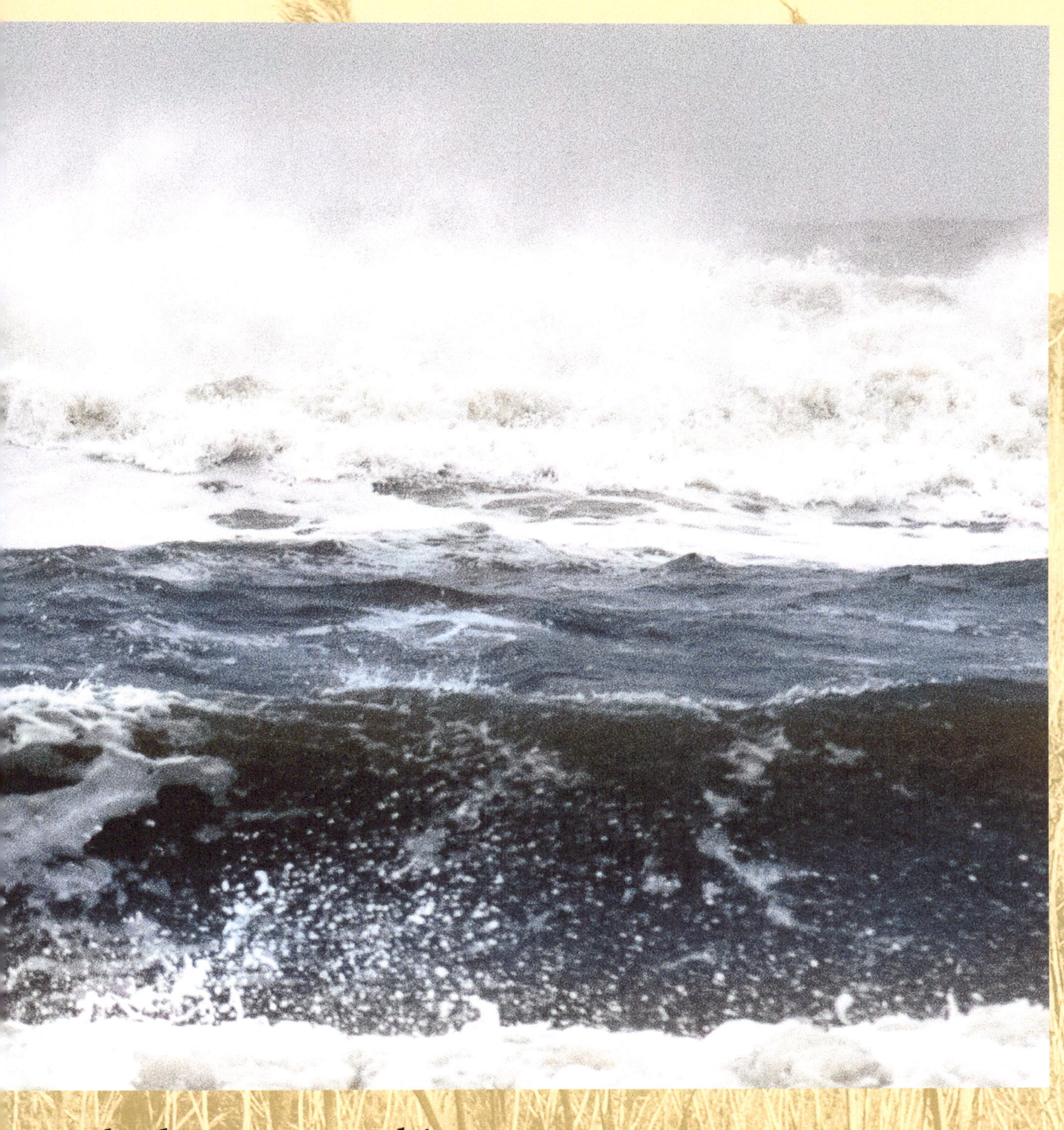

... look pretty rough!

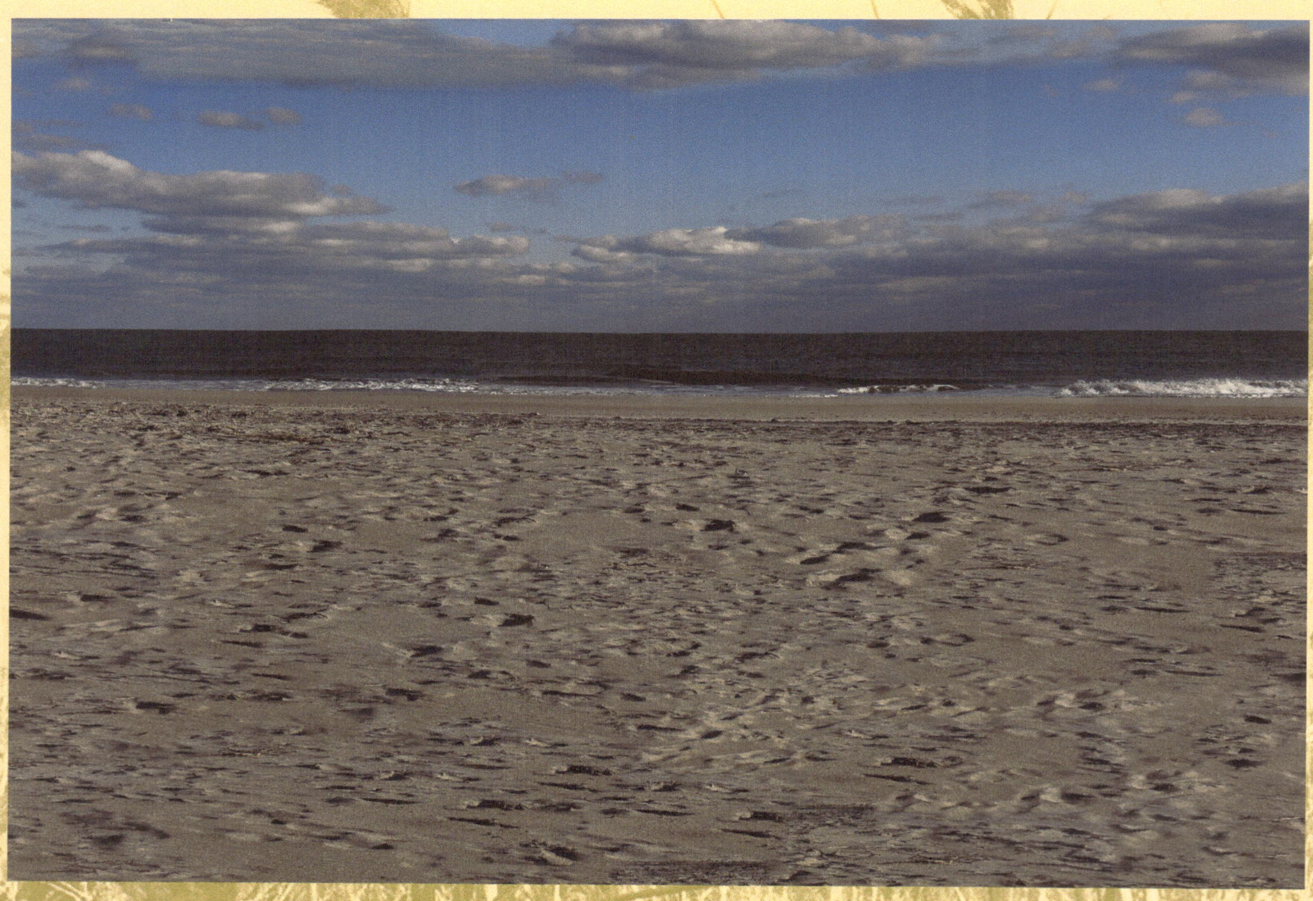

   On another day, though, the beach is sunny and the ocean is totally calm, very unlike its previous temper tantrum.

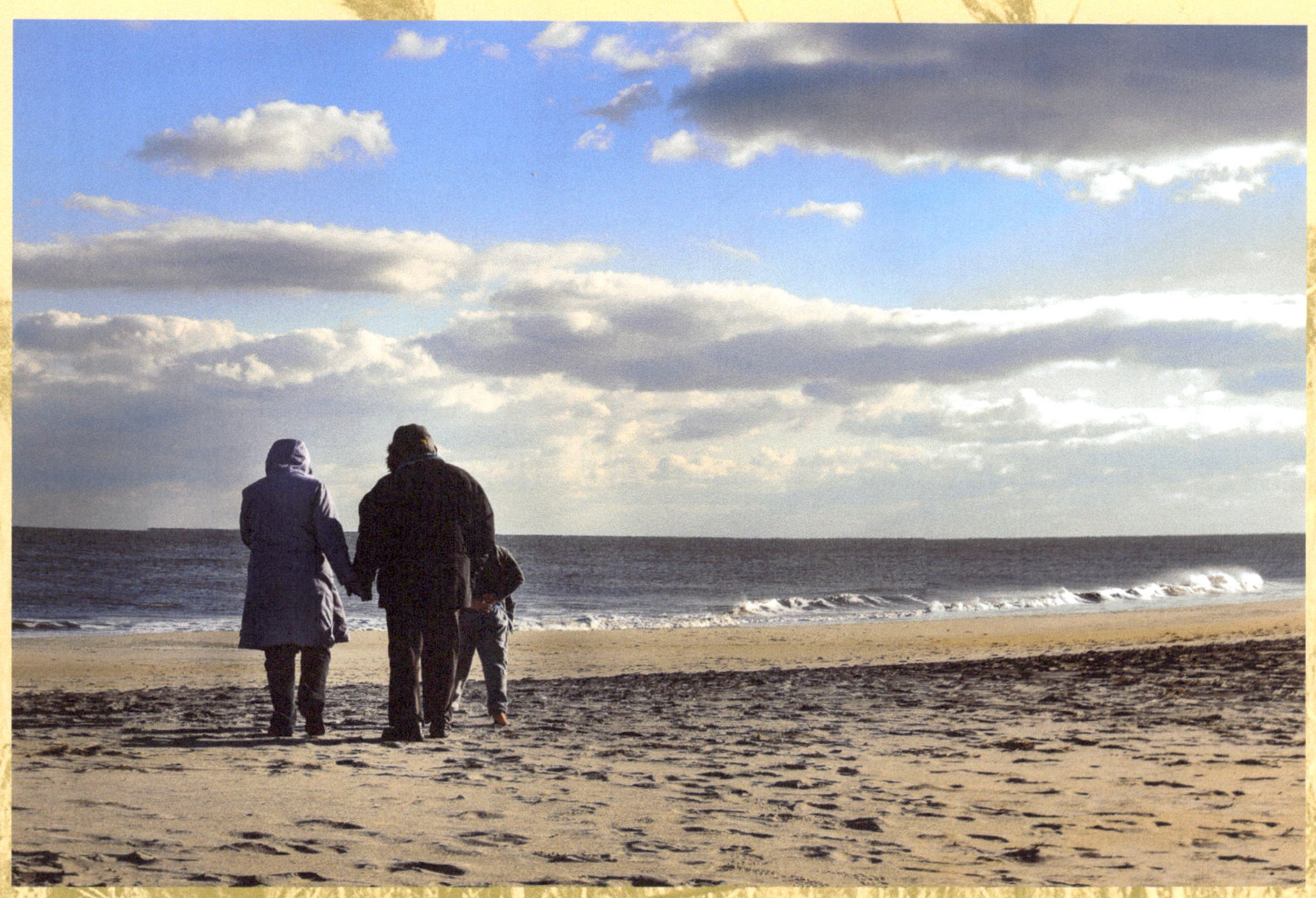

Some people think, however, that the beach is cold and windy, albeit as pretty as can be.

And there are a lot of birds to be enjoyed here too, especially gulls ...

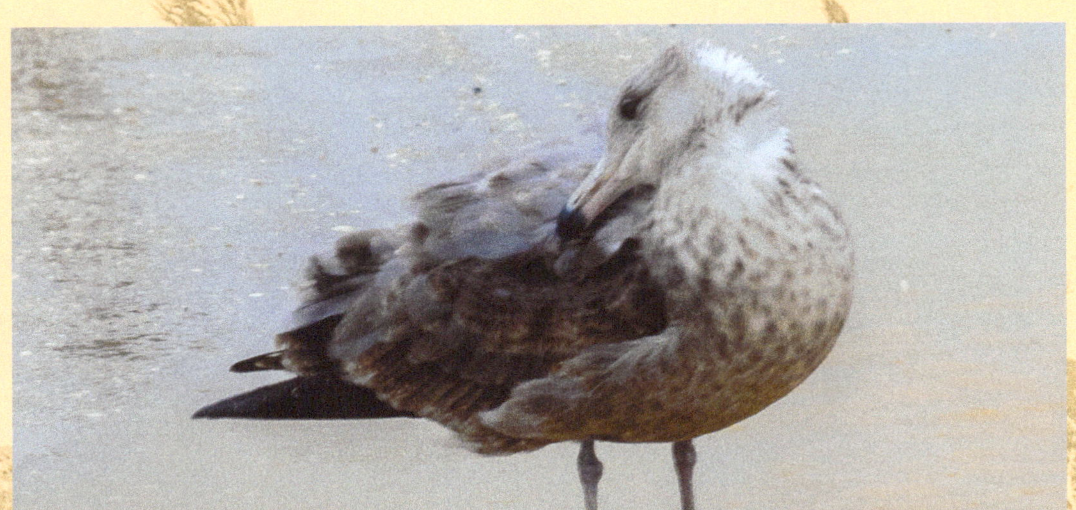

... my goodness, aren't gulls a very common beach bird, and I love them. In a small tidal pool in a beach parking lot, gulls are busy preening, like this first-year ring-billed gull. All birds preen; clean and neat feathers are necessary for their survival.

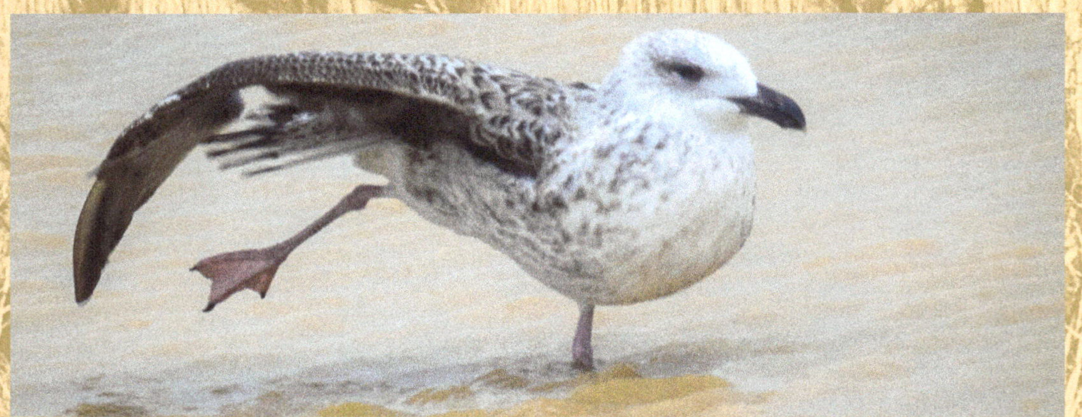

This juvenile great black-backed gull is wing stretching to straighten its feathers—part of its preening routine.

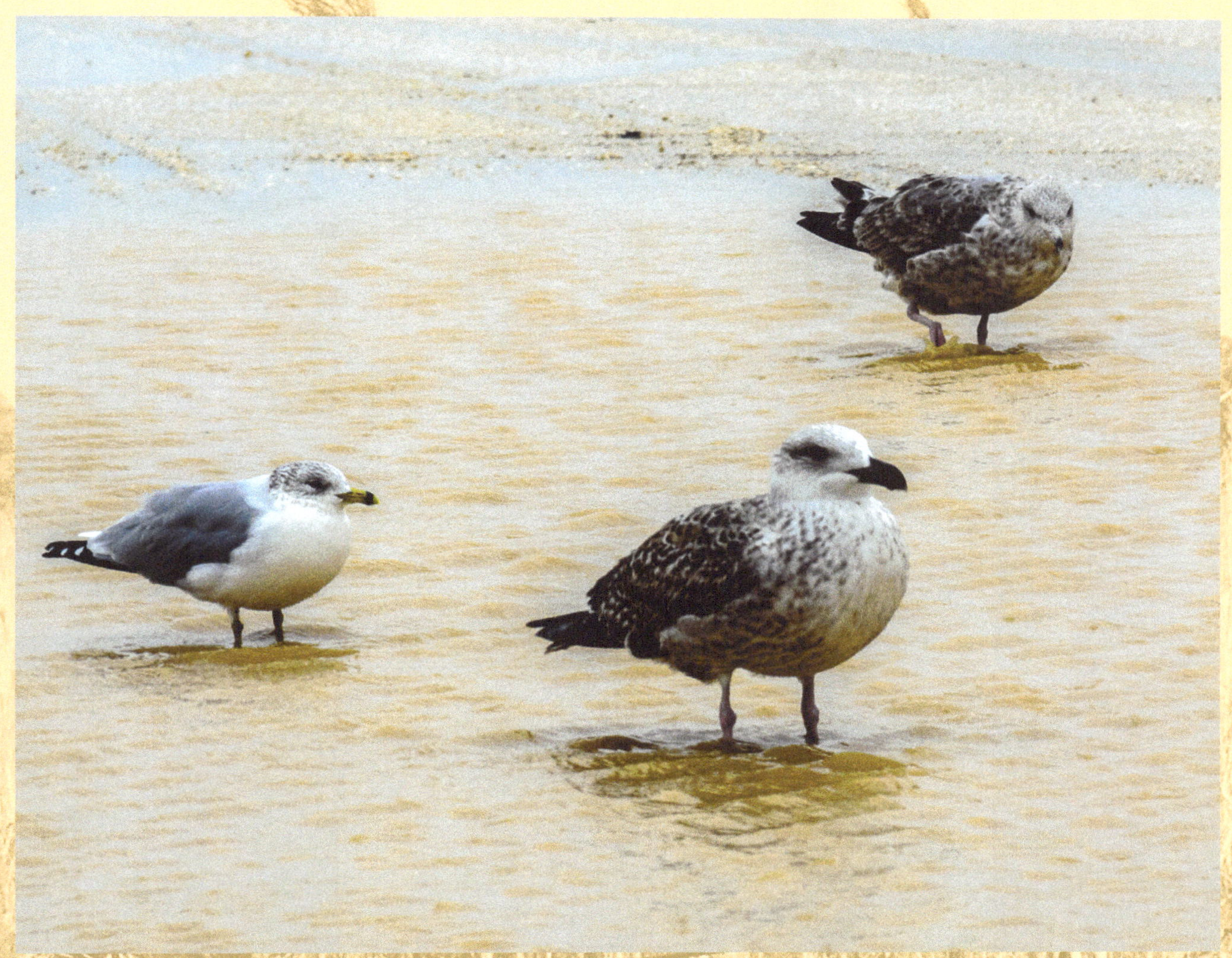

An adult ring-billed gull (left) and a juvenile ring-billed gull (in the back) hang out with a juvenile great black-backed gull (front). Assateague is renowned for its diversity of birds, including, of course, gulls.

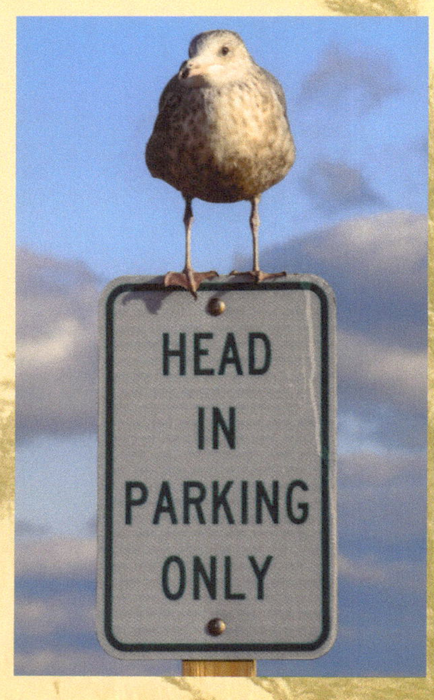

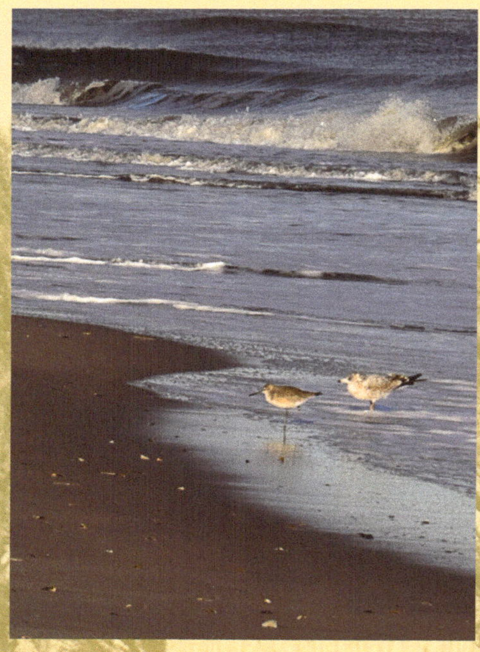

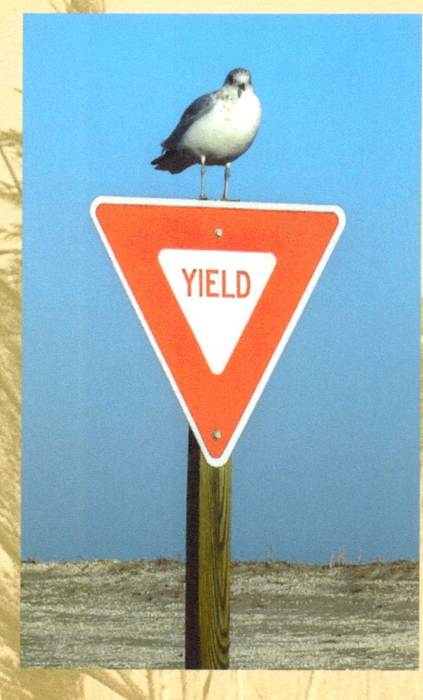

What do birds do at the beach when they're not preening?

Well, there are the beach-bum birds (such as this willet and this juvenile ring-billed gull), as well as hard working gulls enforcing traffic ordinances.

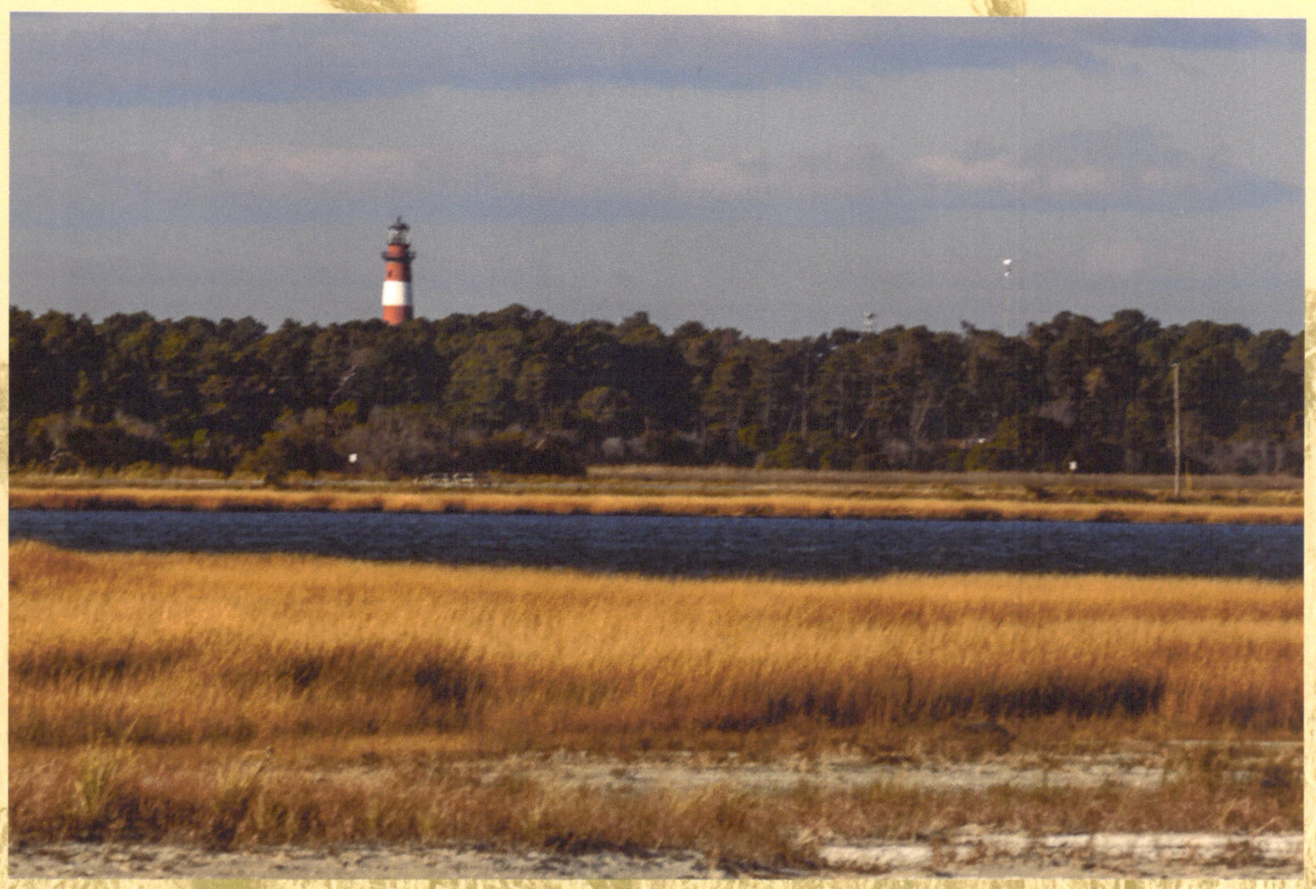

We turn around, look west, and behold! There is the lighthouse, as well as a tidal pool, surrounded by salt marsh cord grass.

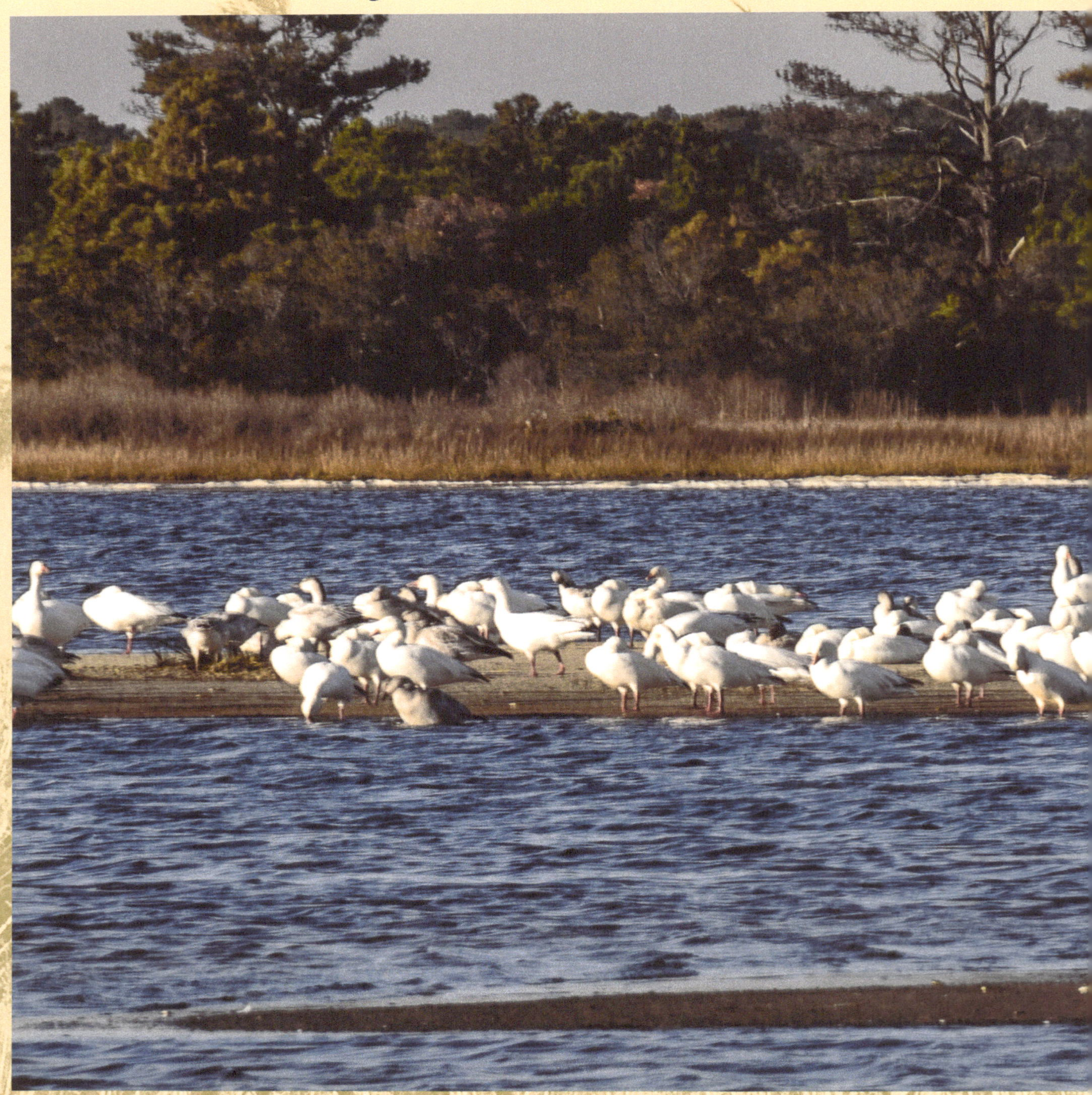

Finally, we find the snow geese. Apparently they no longer care for Snow Goose Pond, in spite of its name,

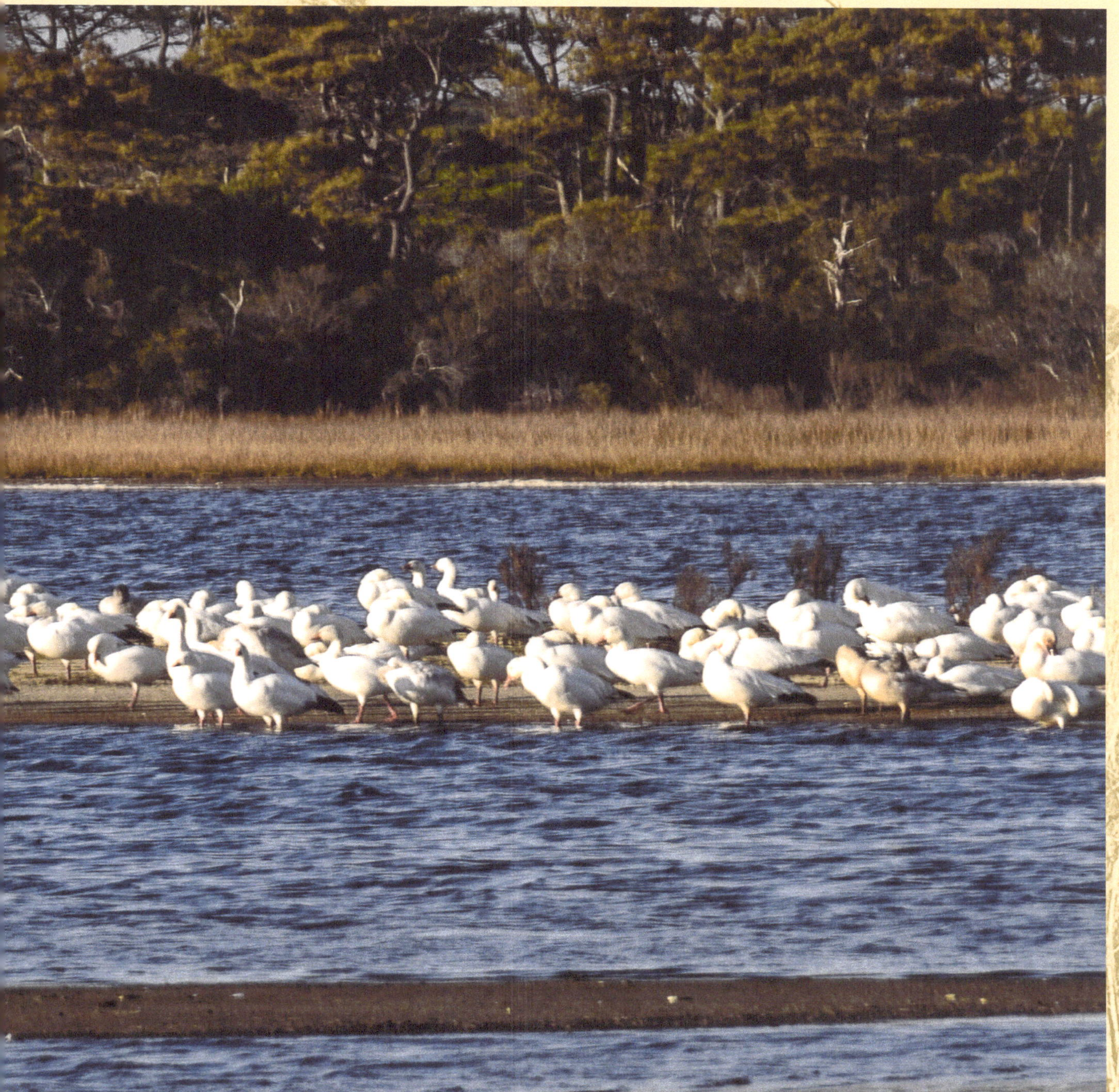

and have now moved to Swan Cove, a tidal pool not far from the ocean. Maybe the air is a little fresher here.

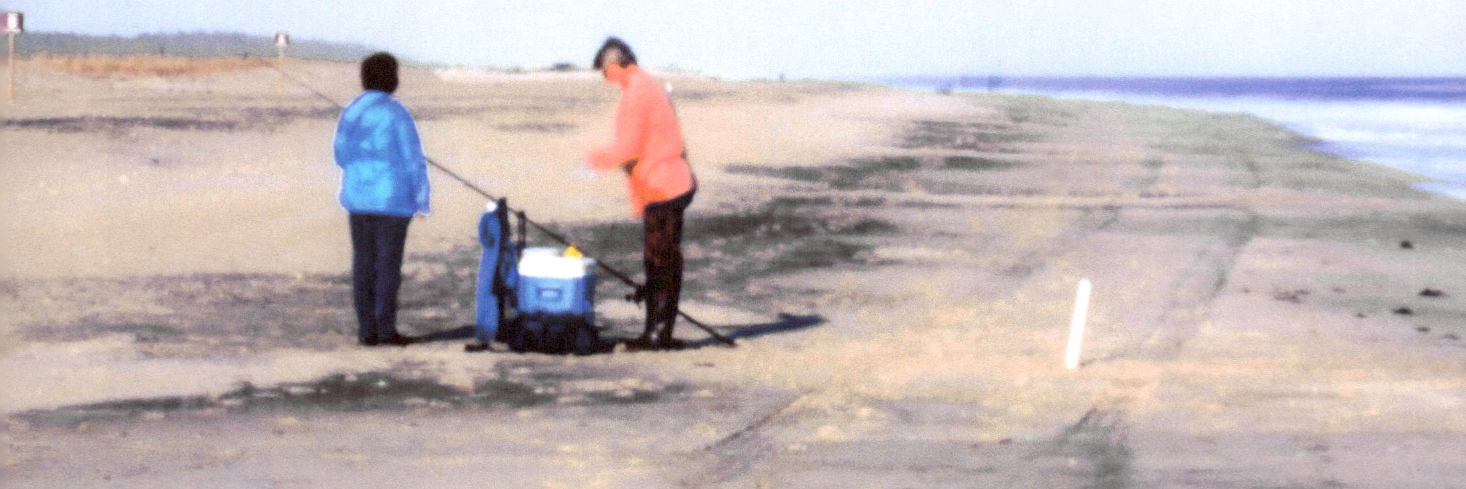

And before we leave, how about a little ocean fishing at the beach on Assateague Island?

Chapter 8 -- We Sadly Say Goodbye

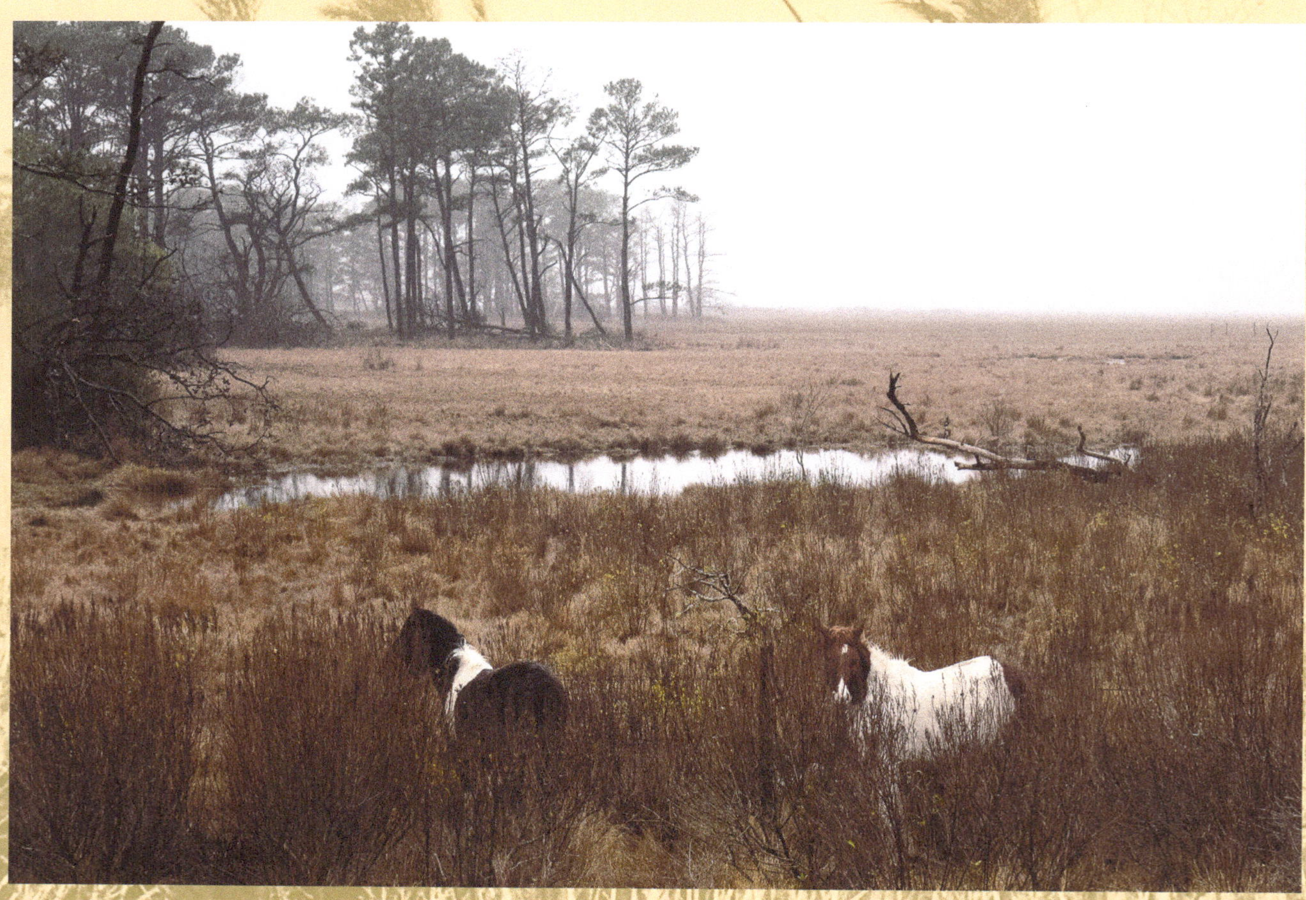

This is the last day of our week visiting Assateague and Chincoteague islands. On a sad and thoroughly overcast day, we visit one last time with our new-found friends. The ponies gaze a fond farewell to us.

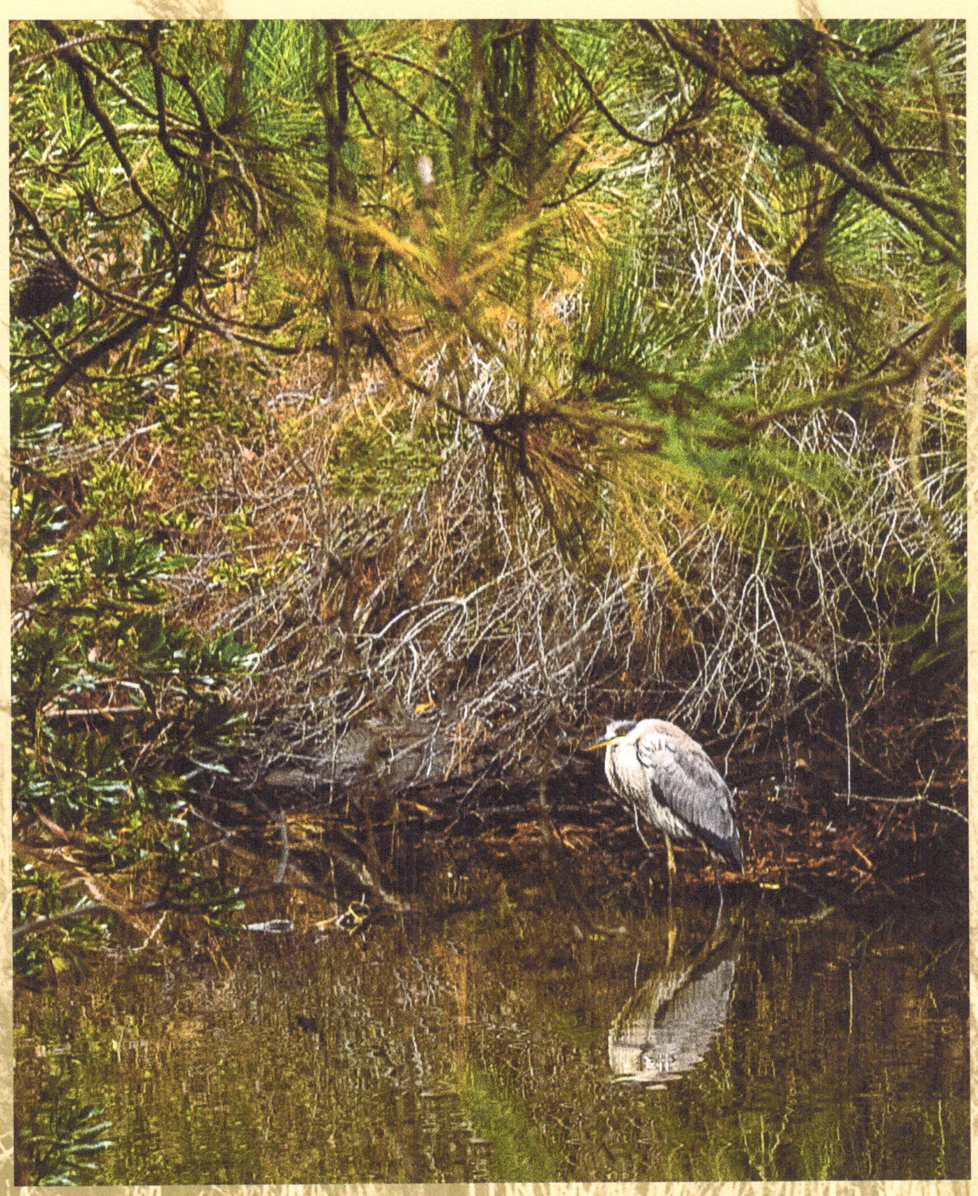

And a great blue heron brooding by
a canal in a pine grove wishes us gone.

We Sadly Say Goodbye

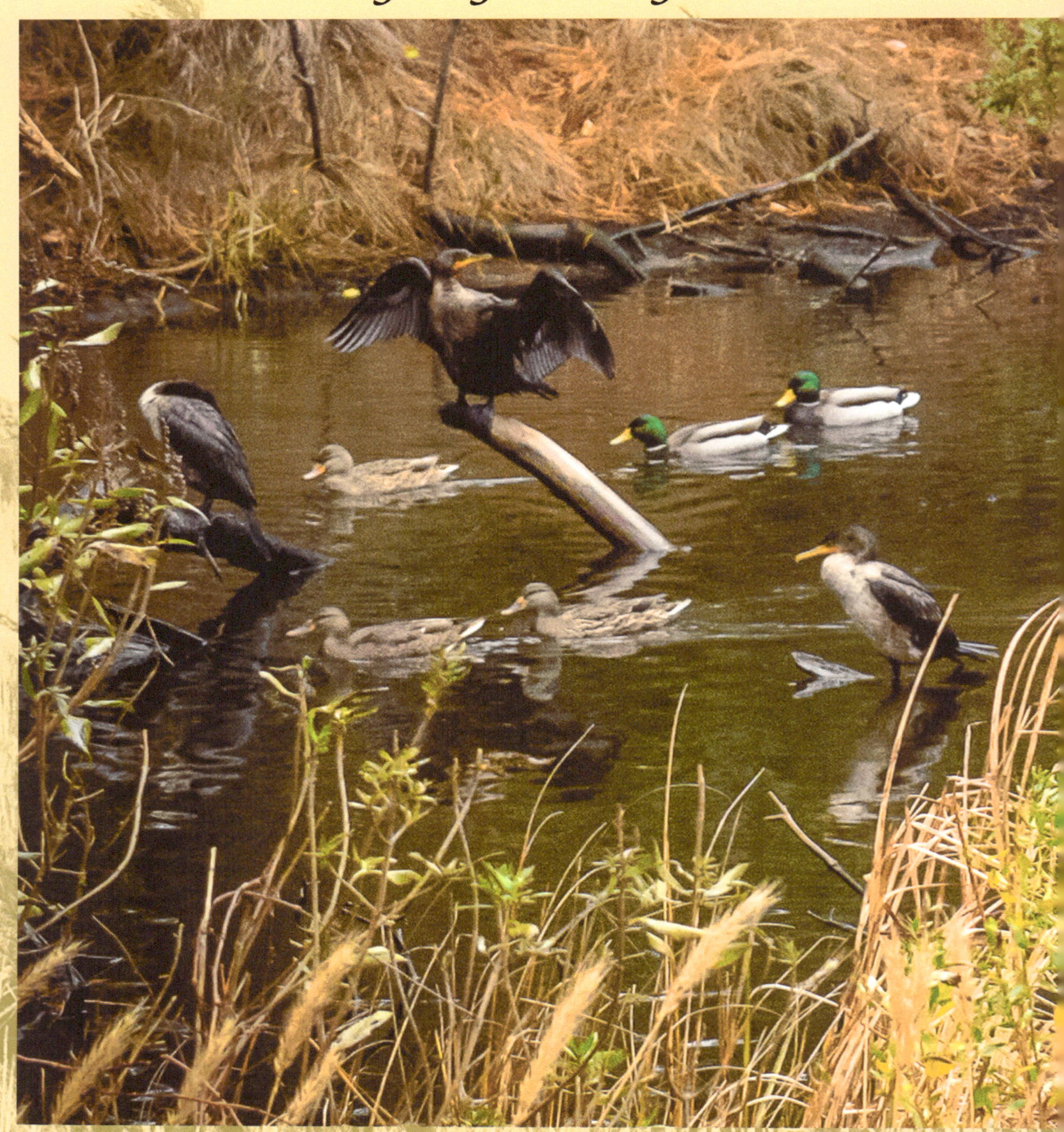

We're already beginning to miss the birds. Here mallard ducks invade the serenity of some double-crested cormorants. Although both

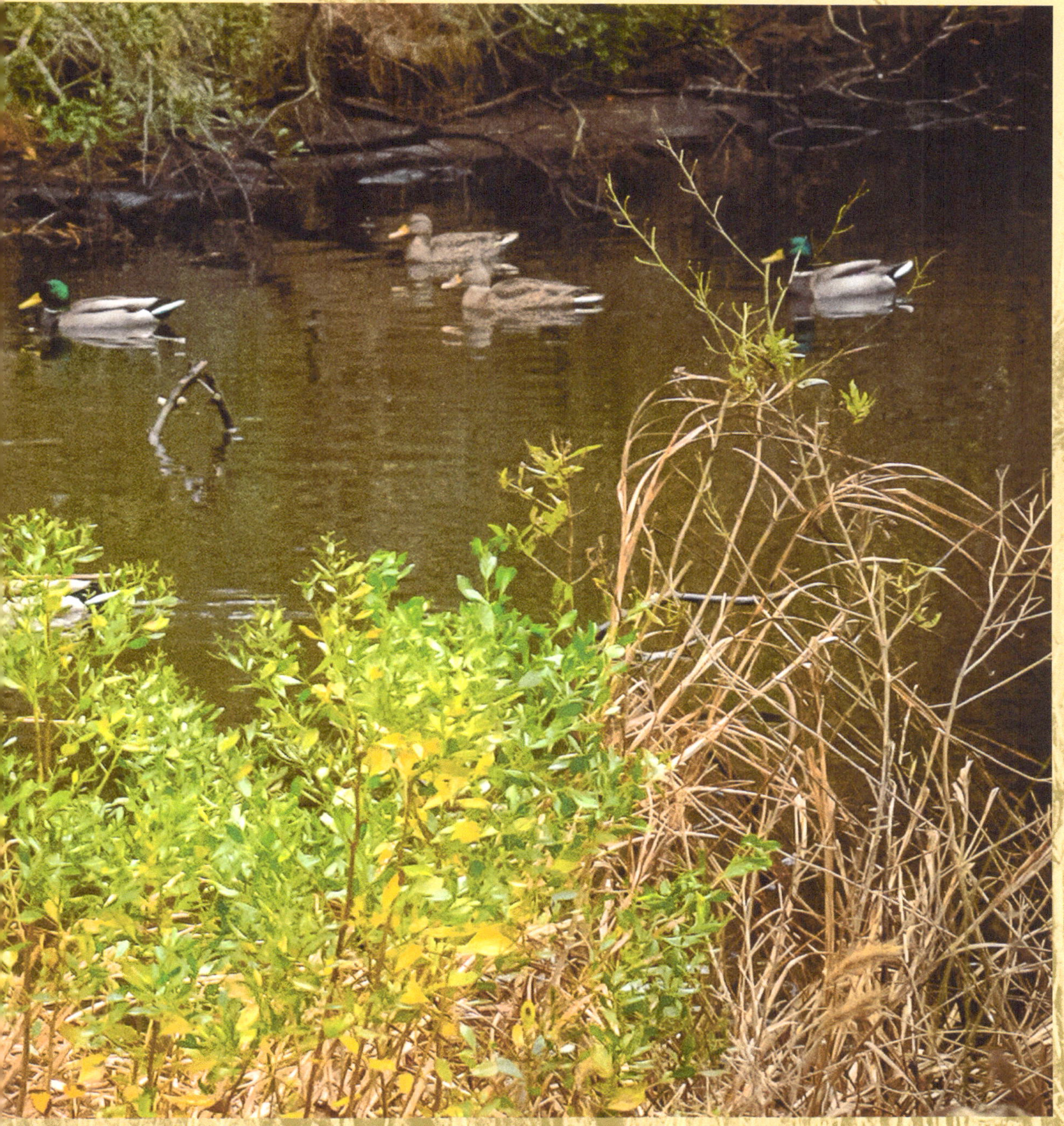

ducks and cormorants are aquatic birds, duck feathers repel water, while cormorant feathers do not. You can see here how one of the cormorants is spreading its wings to dry its feathers.

We Sadly Say Goodbye

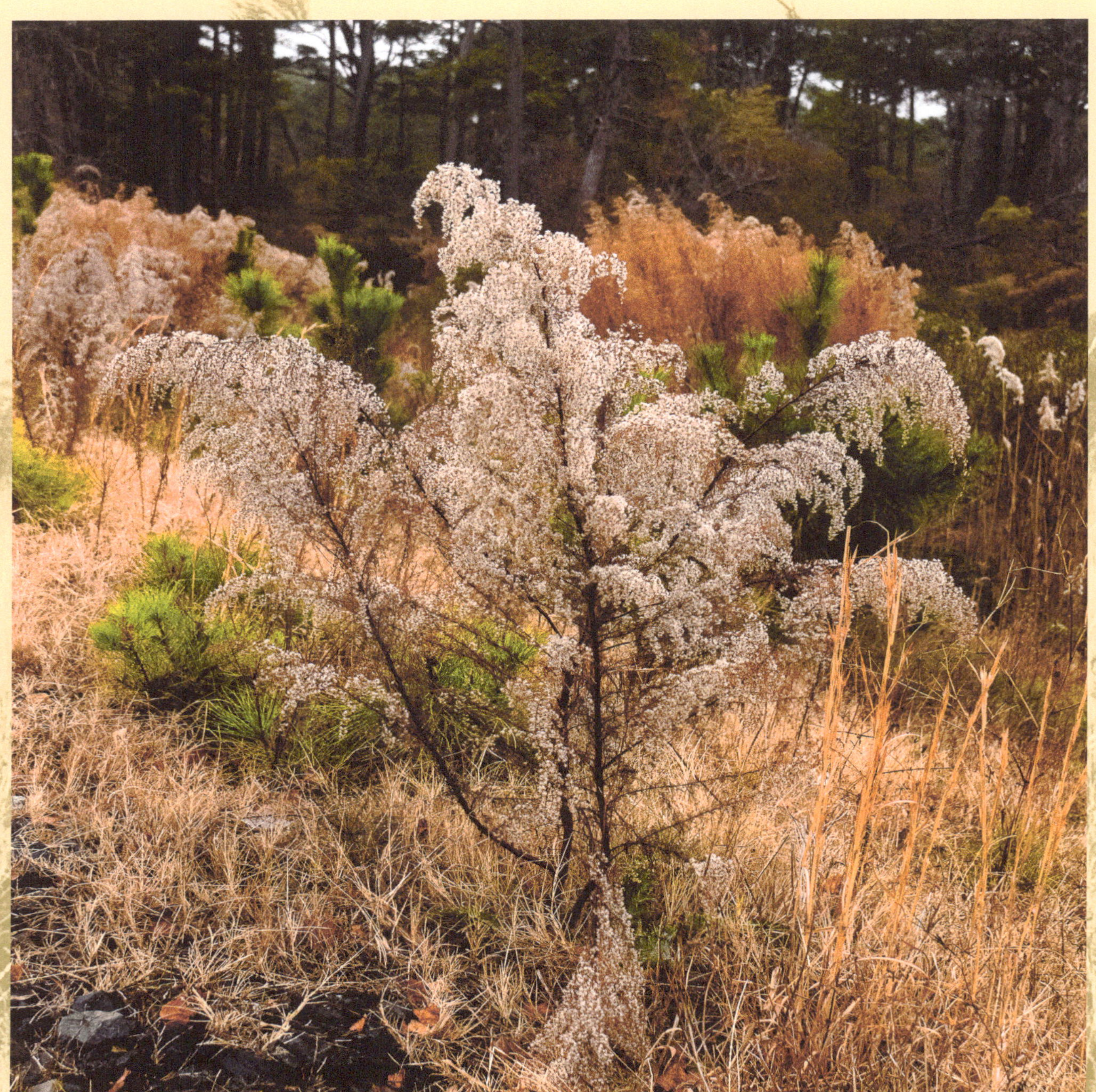

We will `certainly miss the beautiful colors and textures that Assateague Island offers, such as this woolgrass …

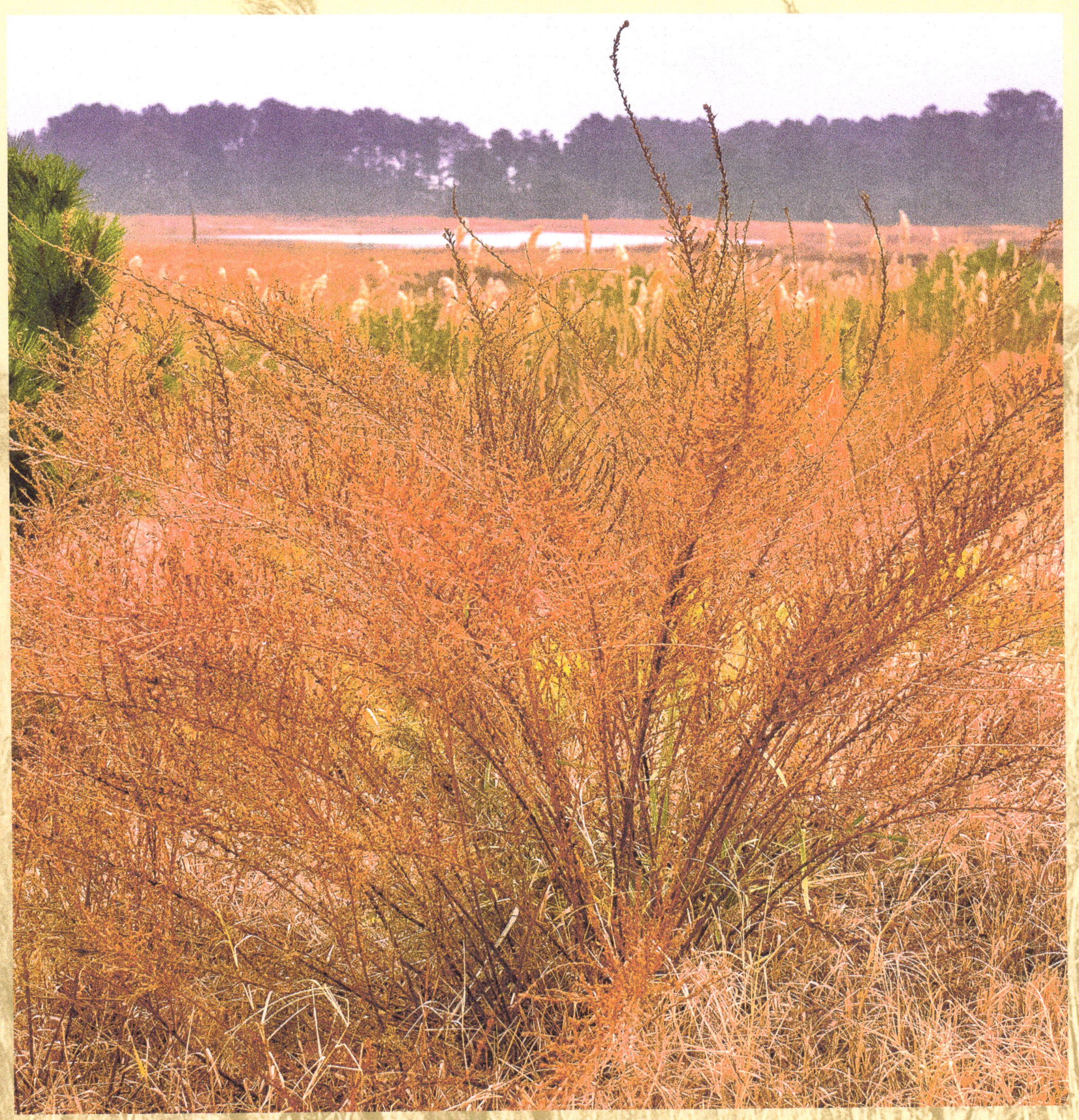

... and this fiery-red saltwort.

   Wistfully, we scan the marshlands thriving with salt marsh cord grass, so full of life in their enormous expanse.

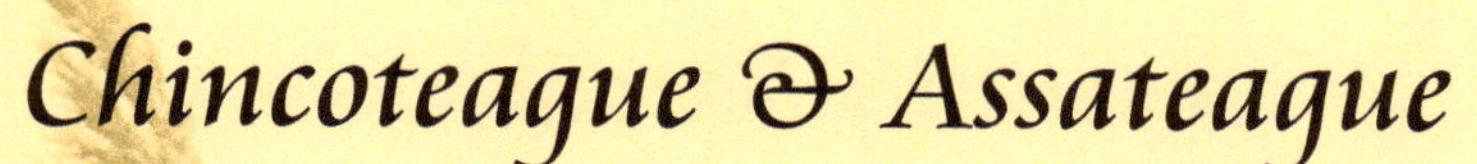

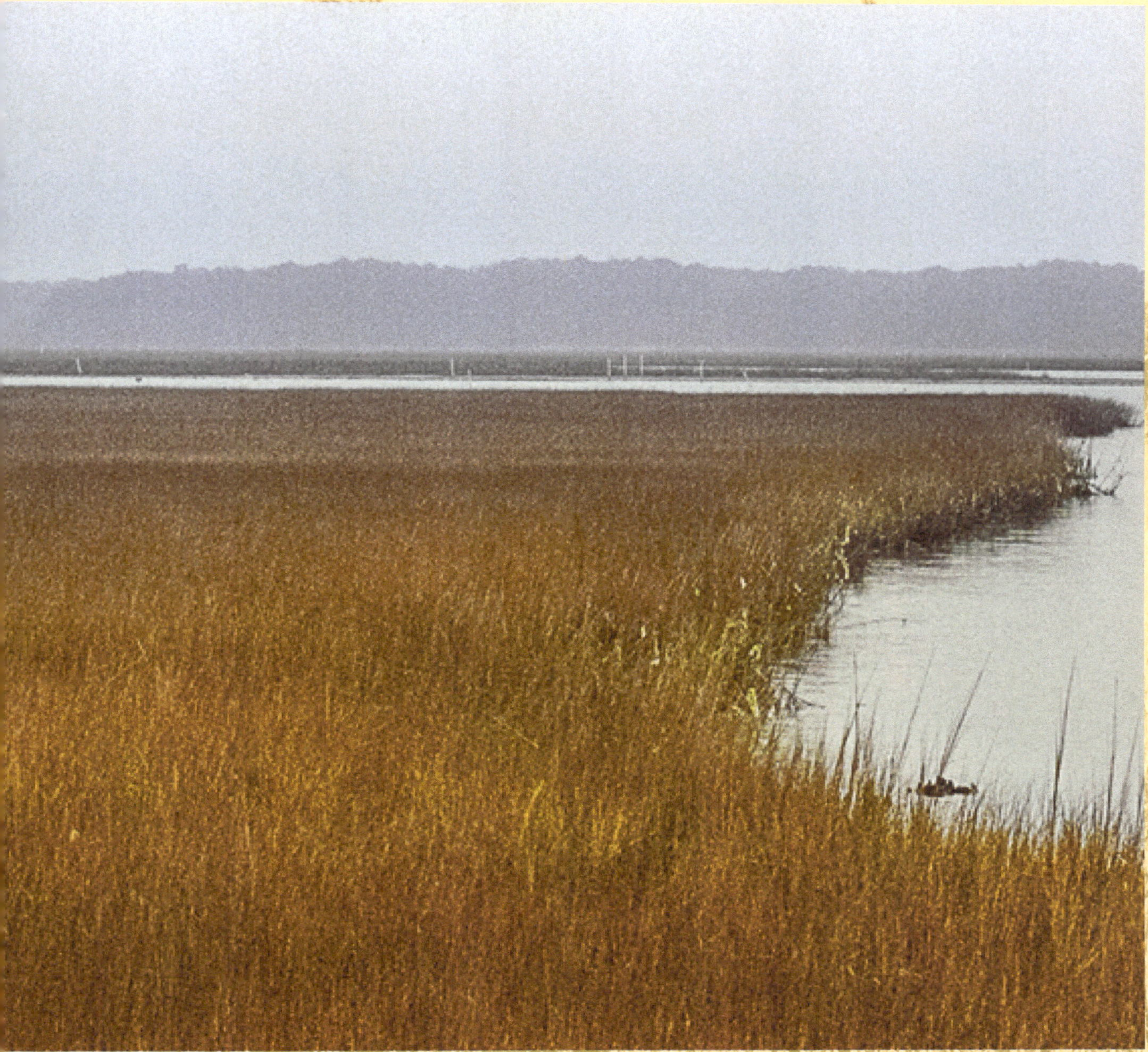

We Sadly Say Goodbye

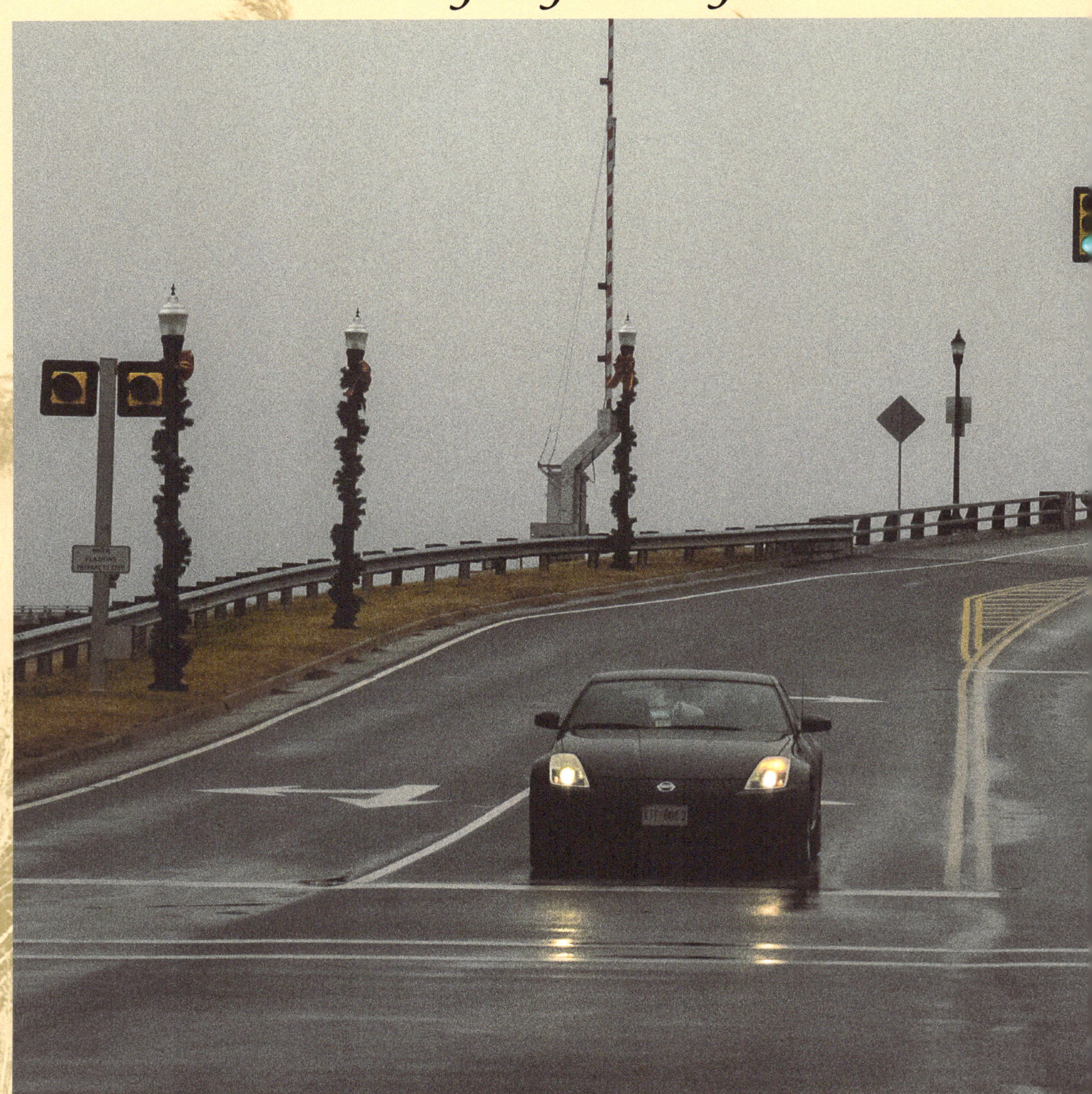

But the time comes to cross the bridge out of Chincoteague Island, and with heavy hearts at having to leave,

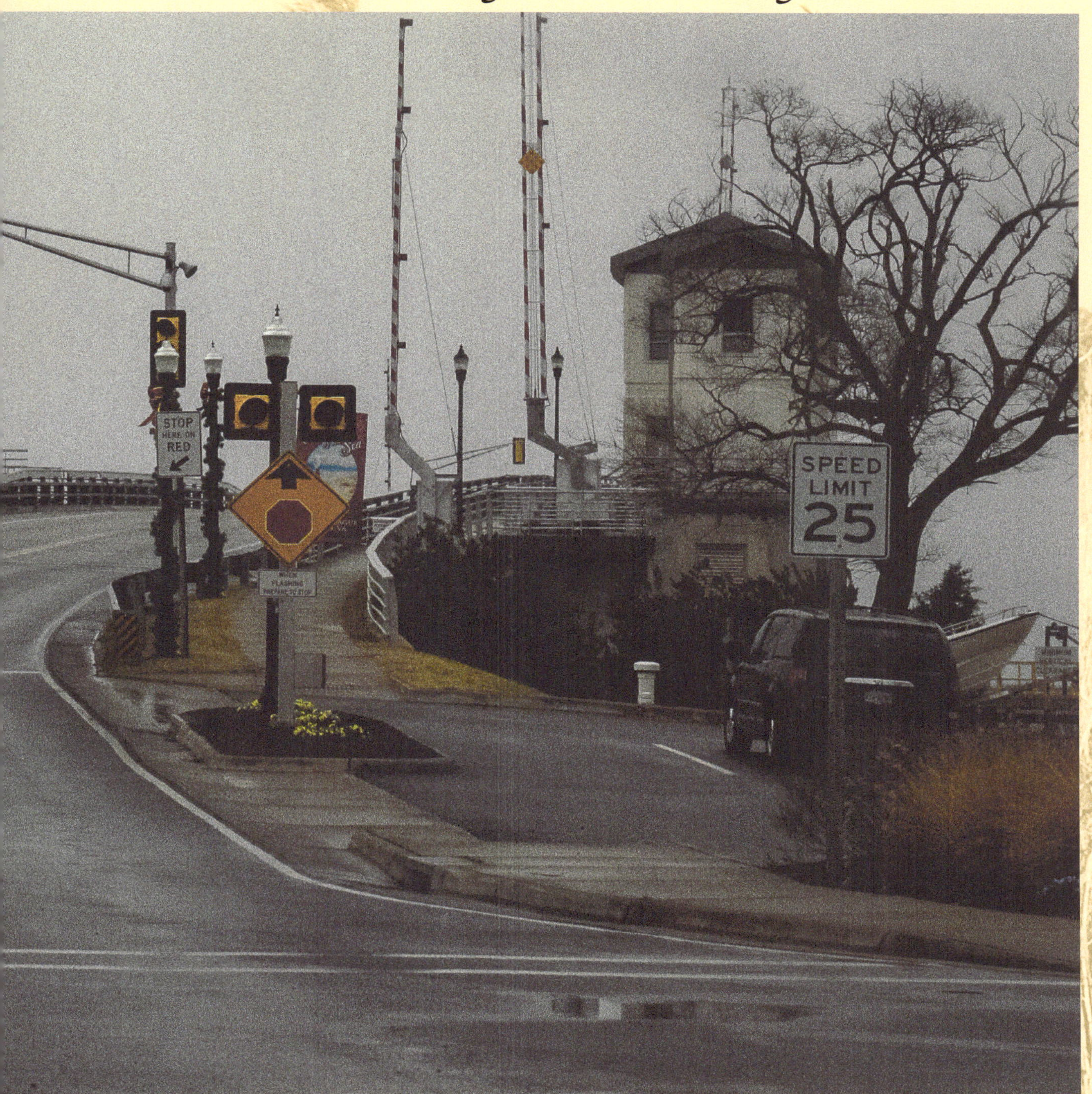

we begin the journey back to the mainland, leaving behind a different world, a world much closer to nature.

Epilogue

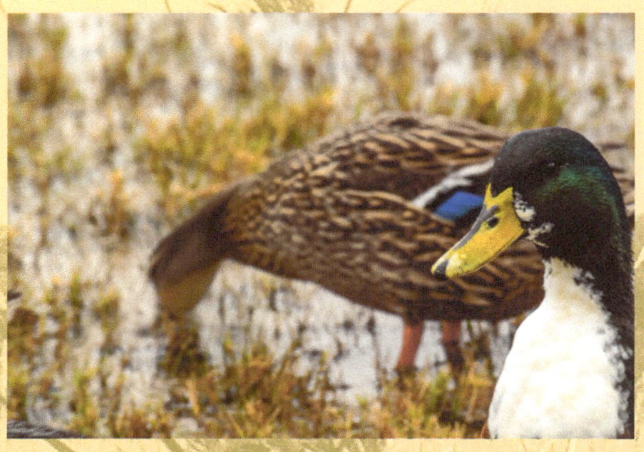

As you can see, my wife and I are practically becoming part of the nature scene. We are really digging into the environment, and eating it up. And that's not just a lot of quacking, my friend.

We'll take wing soon and again join the folks who flock to enjoy these magical islands. Will we be seeing you there?

By the way, tourists, birders, photographers, and weekend naturalists are all abundant on these islands, taking in the sights and excitement of this migratory stopover.

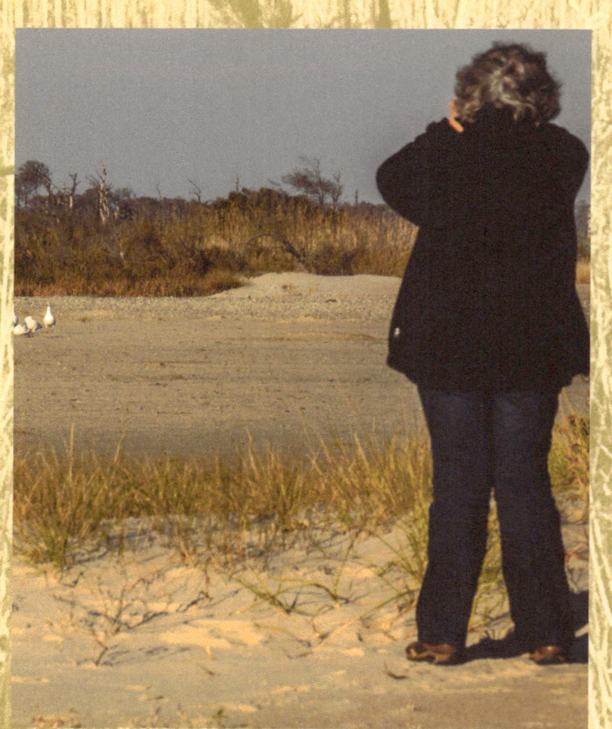

Put yourself in this picture!

And Check Out These Too

- Chincoteague Chamber of Commerce
  www.chincoteaguechamber.com

- Chincoteague website
  www.chincoteague.com

- Pony Swim/Auction: July every year

- Pony Centre, Chicken City Rd, 757-336-2776

- Veteran's Memorial Park,
  Ridge Rd & Memorial Park, very family friendly

- Camping: several sites; may be too buggy for some

- Maria's Restaurant, 6506 Maddox Blvd, 757-336-5040
  Great family style buffet; closed after Thanksgiving

- Chincoteague Island Outfitters (kayaks, bicycles, etc.)
  7885 Eastside Road, 757-336-5129

- Mr. Whippy, Chincoteague's historic source for
  soft ice cream; 6201 Maddox Blvd , 757-336-5122

- Swimming on Assateague beach, with shower facilities
  (Need I say, it's only for the summer)

- Wallops Flight Facility Visitor Center (NASA)
  Route 175 on the way to Chincoteague Island, by the side
  of the road (See this before or after a Chincoteague visit)
  (Family friendly)

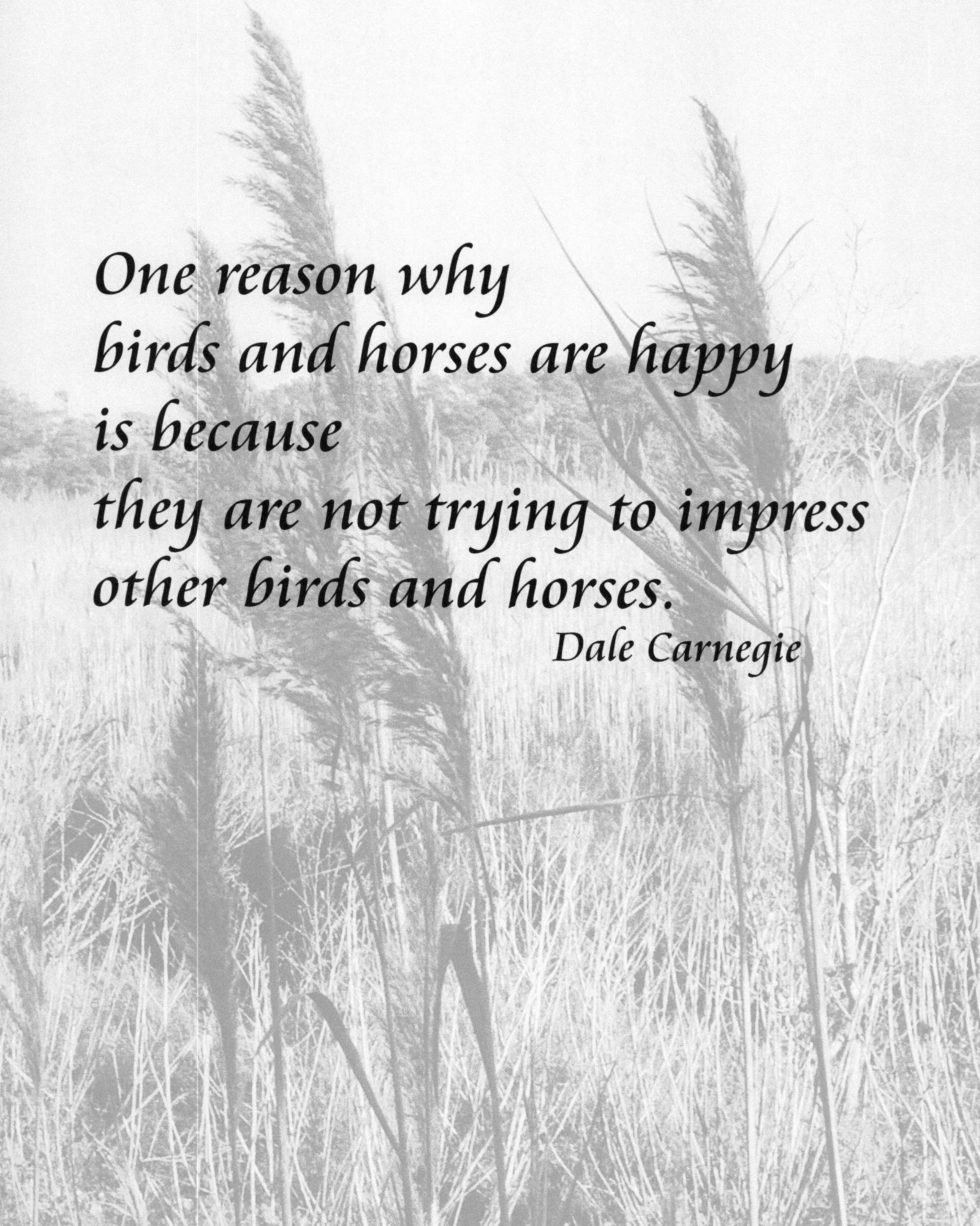

One reason why
birds and horses are happy
is because
they are not trying to impress
other birds and horses.
Dale Carnegie